COLLEGE

REGIONS AND REGIONALISM IN THE UNITED STATES

210

The Contemporary United States

Series Editors: CHRISTOPHER BROOKEMAN AND WILLIAM ISSEL

PUBLISHED TITLES

FORTHCOMING TITLES

REGIONS AND REGIONALISM IN THE UNITED STATES

Michael Bradshaw

MACMILLAN EDUCATION

First published 1988

Published by
MACMILLAN EDUCATION LTD
Houndmills, Basingstoke, Hampshire RG21 2XS
and London
Companies and representatives
throughout the world

Typeset by Wessex Typesetters
(Division of The Eastern Press Ltd)
Frome, Somerset

Printed in Hong Kong

British Library Cataloguing in Publication Data
Bradshaw, Michael
Regions and regionalism in the United
States.—(The Contemporary United States).
1. Regional planning—United States
I. Title   II. Series
361.6′1′0973   HT392
ISBN 0–333–39861–0
ISBN 0–333–39862–9 Pbk

Series Standing Order

If you would like to receive future titles in this series as they are
published, you can make use of our standing order facility. To place a
standing order please contact your bookseller or, in case of difficulty,
write to us at the address below with your name and address and the
name of the series. Please state with which title you wish to begin your
standing order. (If you live outside the United Kingdom we may not
have the rights for your area, in which case we will forward your order
to the publisher concerned.)

Customer Services Department, Macmillan Distribution Ltd
Houndmills, Basingstoke, Hampshire, RG21 2XS, England.

Contents

Preface

This book sets out to provide a study of regional variations within the United States, and a critique of the significance of the regional concept as applied in expressions of regionalism in the US in the middle and later part of the twentieth century. In working towards this aim, I have had to come to terms with changes in the ways that geographers have viewed, and made use of, regions as units for study. The writing of this book has become something of a personal journey, but it is hoped that not only will it be seen as an account of the 'state of the art', but also that some new contributions are made.

My secondary aim is to link academic studies with the 'practical' decision-making of government and business concerns. It stems from a desire to be involved in informing those decisions, as well as from a wish to understand and explain them. Social scientists have been less successful in providing help to the decision-makers than in venting negative criticisms of what has taken place as a result of public policy. This book, dealing with the academic pursuit of regional studies and the public expression of regional hopes through regionalism, provides an opportunity to bring these aspects of social science together.

The arrangement of the book is determined partly by the personal journey, and partly by the assumption that some readers may be new to a study of the geography or regional study of the United States. The reader is provided with a knowledge of the different parts of the United States, which increases in depth and detail through the book. The logic of the argument followed is designed to examine developments within the field of regional geography, and then to apply the approach to an examination of regionalism within the US. General points are drawn from this study at the end. The publishers have allowed me to include a range of maps and diagrams to illustrate the text, and these are used to introduce detailed information instead of expanding the text with long listy descriptions.

No book is merely the product of one person's thinking, although I take responsibility for the views expressed and the manner in which they are developed. I thank the series editors, Chris Brookeman and Bill Issel, for asking me to write the book and for continuing encouragement. A number of American friends who have been closely involved in public policy regionalism in the United States have provided me with insights and information, and have been unstinting in their giving of time for discussion: Mike Wenger, John Whisman and especially Don Whitehead have my grateful thanks. This book has also gained from discussion of some of the issues developed here over a number of years with Professor John Paterson and Dr Roland Allison. Tony Atkin has drawn the diagrams.

Plymouth, 1986   MICHAEL BRADSHAW

Editors' Preface

Mention the United States and few people respond with feelings of neutrality. Discussions about the role of the United States in the contemporary world typically evoke a sense of admiration or a shudder of dislike. Pundits and politicians alike make sweeping references to attributes of modern society deemed 'characteristically American'. Yet qualifications are in order, especially regarding the distinctiveness of American society and the uniqueness of American culture. True, American society has been shaped by the size of the country, the migratory habits of the people and the federal system of government. Certainly, American culture cannot be understood apart from its multi-cultural character, its irreverence for tradition and its worship of technological imagery. It is equally true, however, that life in the United States has been profoundly shaped by the dynamics of American capitalism and by the penetration of capitalist market imperatives into all aspects of daily life.

The series is designed to take advantage of the growth of specialised research about post-war America in order to foster understanding of the period as a whole as well as to offer a critical assessment of the leading developments of the post-war years. Coming to terms with the United States since 1945 requires a willingness to accept complexity and ambiguity, for the history encompasses conflict as well as consensus, hope as well as despair, progress as well as stagnation. Each book in the series offers an interpretation designed to spark discussion rather than a definite account intended to close debate. The series as a whole is meant to offer students, teachers and the general public fresh perspectives and new insights about the contemporary United States.

CHRISTOPHER BROOKEMAN
WILLIAM ISSEL

ix

PART I: REGIONAL DIFFERENCES

1. The Significance of Regions

1.1 INTRODUCTION: REGIONS AND REGIONALISM

This book is being written at a significant point in the history of studies of regions and regionalism, particularly with reference to the United States. Regions are subnational units of variable size, but within the United States typically comprise parts of all or several states. Studies of social issues within the US have an essential spatial context which is often important at the regional level. Practical solutions to these issues at government and business levels are based on regional units. The present challenge is to bring together the work in regional studies within the social sciences and the actions taken in the 'practical world'.

In the realm of academic enquiry there is a strong development of emphases on these regional units within American Studies, bringing together literature, the visual arts and historical accounts in terms of 'regional images'. At the same time, geographers – who have focused on regional units as a basis for study – are reassessing their approaches to regional studies as a central part of their discipline.

Since the 1960s there has also been an increasing trend in government and business in the United States to acknowledge the subnational, or regional, nature of many planning problems. The Federal government reports census statistics in relation to clearly defined regions (Figure 1.1), and many of its agencies use these or other regional divisions as a basis for administering their programmes. \The growth of region-based interest groups\ (regionalism) has led to informal pressures on politicians and, occasionally, to the formal institutionalisation of public policy on a regional basis. The business world organises the territory of the

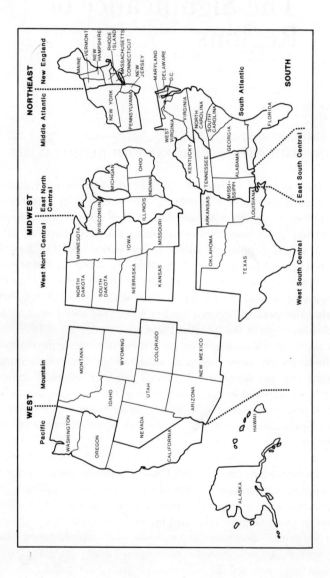

nation into marketing regions, and establishes regional headquarters. This study of regions and regionalism in the United States provides an opportunity to bring these strands together.

1.2 GEOGRAPHERS AND REGIONS

The discipline of geography has had the greatest involvement with the study of regional units. Regional studies formed the basis of the efforts of geographers up to the 1950s to identify and account for differences in human usage of the earth's surface. Such studies provided much that was useful and interesting to the general public, business and government departments (Hart, 1982). However, many geographers came to the conclusion that these studies were merely descriptions of unique sections of the earth's surface: the study of one region held little of value to contribute to the study of other regions. This type of regional study has recently been linked with the commercial geography and political geography which were popular in the first half of the twentieth century. Geographical studies in this vein are described as having been more appropriate in the bygone age of European empires and commercial colonialism (Smith, 1984). At that stage it was important to know the detailed distributions of the production of major commodities, and those of physical environments to which production might be extended. In the mid 1980s there is less confidence in the 'explanations' based on simple links between the natural environment and human activities.

To replace this largely descriptive approach, there was a move in the 1960s and early 1970s to establish a more 'scientific' geography based on economic models and quantitative methods of analysis. This approach attempted to formulate general rules, or norms, which could be used to predict change in the economy and so to inform planning decisions. It tended to emphasise processes at work, and resulted in the more rapid development of systematic

---

FIGURE 1.1 The four Regions and nine Divisions of the United States recognised by the Bureau of Census. Census data are summarised on this basis, but other US government departments use different bases for their regions

aspects of geographical study (economic, urban) at the expense of regional aspects. The trouble with this approach was that it proved difficult to apply models, such as those related to regional development, in planning (e.g. the growth centre concept, Friedmann and Weaver, 1979). Also:

> The domain of this spatial science was a silent, subterranean world of point patterns and networks, whose underlying 'order' was undisturbed by the babble of jostling and joking human beings. (Gregory, 1985)

Attempts to avoid this divorce from the reality of human experience led to the adoption of concepts from behavioural psychology to explain the rules of locational choice. However, this provided yet another partial view of societies which did not take into account much of the complexity and even ambiguity of human agency.

The attention of geographers in the later 1970s was transferred to more humanistic approaches based on attempts to understand the meanings behind human actions ('the babble of jostling human beings'), rather than on the goal of explaining the general features of geographical settings. The latter had tended to lead to deterministic economic explanations, which excluded the influence of individuals. Geographers began to move from being external and neutral observers of the world in which they lived to becoming more involved in society and social change.

Regional geography is finding a new base within this humanistic framework, and this shift also has the effect of placing it at the centre of social science enquiry (Lee, 1985). The base involves interactions of individual and group activities both with their natural environment and also with social structures. These interactions take place at particular places and within particular regions, thus emphasising the 'real' world, as opposed to the idealistic (and often simplistic) generalisations of 'scientific' geography. The interactions also vary over time, since the social structures established by one culture become modified by individuals and groups, who also interact in different ways with the natural environment. The human activities within each culture (economic, social, political) produce artefacts of buildings, settlements, field patterns, transport routes. The combination of the artefacts and activities provides a region with its distinctive 'geography' at any period of time. Regional geographies are not static, but change over time in nature and emphasis. Each new geography carries forward elements of the past, which may be used in new ways, or left as redundant reminders of the past. The geography of a region is thus cumulative and always subject to the prospect of change. A region – along with other geographical units at different scales (local, global) – becomes a vehicle for the application of geographical ideas and methods, and for uniting varied approaches in an overall view of human societies.

Traditionally, a 'region' has been defined as a tract of land with relatively homogeneous characteristics and marked boundaries. Such a definition has commonly led to the drawing of boundaries along features of the natural environment, such as mountain ranges and rivers. This has had the effect of imbuing the boundaries with a false permanence, and of emphasising the interactions between people living inside the region and their natural environment. The region becomes a rather introspective entity, while the importance of social structures and inter-regional linkages are minimised. And yet almost every boundary defined in this way can be disputed, and different geographers may use different bases for drawing boundaries across the same territory. In addition, although it may once have been possible to identify relatively homogeneous and unique regional tracts within the US, the increasing mobility of the later twentieth century has brought a greater uniformity to the nation, and has emphasised the growing importance of inter-regional links, together with that of social and political structures. New attempts to adopt a regional base for geographical study have to accommodate these trends.

Regions are not isolated geographical entities, but parts of a national and international system of inter-relating sections of the earth's surface. Regions can also be divided into smaller, local, units. As the relationships between these levels of spatial organisation change, so a particular region may change from growth to decline, from core to periphery, in its economic and political status. Within each region there is an accumulation of relict features from the different regional geographies established over time: each phase of history leaves behind a little or much to posterity and helps to affect the nature of the next stage of the evolving region.

In this way regional studies are based on dynamic concepts,

involving a developing interaction between people and their locations, and being subject to changes of emphasis over time. Regions of the US with a longer history of settlement by European-origin cultures (i.e. the east coast) will have a different human geography from those settled more recently (i.e. much of the West) by virtue of the greater number of historic 'relics' still present in the landscape – as well as the interactions with the contrasting physical geographies (Stilgoe, 1982).

'Regionalism' is another aspect of this dynamic view. It involves the belief that a regional solution may be found for social, economic or political problems, and often results from a community of interest or embattled position in time of economic hardship or political stress. The Confederacy believed that it had to secede from the Union in 1861, since the regional interests of the southern planters appeared to be in danger at the time of the election of Abraham Lincoln as president of the US. A hundred years later, a consortium of state governors persuaded the Kennedy administration in the early 1960s that the problems of the Appalachian region were so great that they merited special action. In the late 1970s the businessmen and legislators of the north-eastern states of the US gathered to promote the fortunes of the much-maligned 'Frostbelt'. In each of these cases a regional consciousness led to the organisation of interests and to co-ordinated political action in a variety of ways.

Once such a dynamic view of regions is adopted, and the concept is linked to that of regionalism by a consideration of the processes involved in the evolution of regional entities and concerns, a tool is made available for unlocking some of the major problems facing society today. In this way an academic study may begin to understand and inform the decision-makers in government and business.

1.3 IMAGES OF REGIONS IN THE UNITED STATES

Regions may also be identified in the US in relation to different perceptions of the peoples who inhabit different sections of the nation, of the landscapes which are lived in or visited, or of the way in which territory may be organised for some business or government end. Such perceived regions do not conflict with the new geographical approach to the study of regions and regionalism. They are central to it. The emphasis is on people's views of the places they live in and of other places which they visit or have to relate to in some way. Each part of the nation is viewed comparatively to other parts. People and landscapes are usually the focus of such images.

Differences between parts of the United States can be approached through the stereotypes which have emerged concerning their peoples. There is the Yankee from New England with commerce as their main interest and a rather clipped accent. There is the easy-going southern white speaking in a sing-song drawl. There is the dour mid-westerner with limited, small-town horizons. There is the boasting Texan with the ten-gallon hat. And there is the way-out Californian, forging ahead into new fields hardly imagined by others. Such stereotypes all contain elements of the truth, but are all dangerous generalisations which are often perpetuated by the need for rapid characterisation in the media. The dangers are illustrated by the low view of black people portrayed in Hollywood films up to the 1960s. It is not the 'average', or some distinctive type, which is necessarily the really important consideration within the population of a region, but the total mix.

The traveller across the US meets many landscapes, and each one appears to have an interminable extent! A day spent driving across the coastal plain of North Carolina, or several days across the flat Midwest, is sufficient to convince one of the extent of particular landscapes. And yet passage through the Appalachians or across the western cordilleras provides a wealth of contrasts. Impressions of the varied American landscapes may be gained from personal experiences of residing in, or visiting, the different parts of the country, or through other media, such as literature, films or TV. They help to initiate and amplify images of the regions, to which fashionable preferences are attached. Such preferences are reflected in inter-regional migrations of people. At different times New York, California and Florida have become 'magnets', while other regions, such as the interior prairie grasslands in the nineteenth century, or Appalachia in the mid twentieth century, have had a negative image. Once attained, such popular images are difficult to lose, although major changes may have occurred. Thus, the prairie grasslands acquired the image of being a desert, but were soon found to afford rich farmland in the nineteenth century; New England was regarded as a depressed industrial region, and many found it difficult to adjust this image in the light of 'high-tech' economic growth in the 1970s; and the Mountain West was seen as an isolated and arid periphery, but then changed to a place of attractive amenity and population growth by the 1980s.

The perceptions held by businesses and government agencies concerning the ways in which the vast territory of the United States may be organised for distributing goods and administration constitute another important aspect of regional images. The determination of such regions and their boundaries may be a matter of justification by quantified (so-called 'objective') criteria, or may be more subjective and related to such factors as political pressures or personal understanding of the different parts of the United States.

As with the basic tenets of regional study based on geographical and historical elements, so the emphasis on images has practical outcomes as well as academic interest. It is on the basis of an understanding of the personal views of regional issues, as well as the substantive details of regional variations, that the best practical decisions can be taken.

1.4 CONCLUSIONS

In whatever way people come to a study of the US, they are met by the need to adopt a region-based approach. Although some aspects of the social and economic life can be studied satisfactorily at national level, there is also a richness of regional variety which can inform planning, marketing and personal locational decisions. However, there is a need to relate the study of regions within the US to something more tangible and systematic than stereotypes of people, images of landscapes or commercial/political views of what are useful regional divisions. A geographical approach to regional analysis can provide a more objective framework against which other types of regional division, or the statements of regionalism, may be judged.

The development of this approach is begun in Chapter 2 through what may appear to be a more traditional description of the geographical 'elements' of regional differences, seen as distributions of natural resources and people. The limitations of this type of approach are considered. The development from this basic position continues in Chapter 3, where a further dimension of regional analysis is provided in relation to changes over time: at each stage in the historical development of the United States the conditions of interaction between human beings and their natural and social environments have been reflected in distinctive arrangements of regional geography. Each stage has left a legacy of ideas and artefacts for the next, and so regional patterns have not only changed, but one set has influenced that which follows. Different levels of institutional and morphological inertia have been built into the sequences experienced in the various parts of the nation. At each stage the legacy interacts with the human agencies at work and produces further changes. Chapter 4 addresses the nature of region-producing processes which are operating in the late twentieth century, and queries the significance of regional analysis in relation to the apparently increasing 'sameness' of American cultural life in the mid 1980s.

The second part of the book focuses on the concerns of regionalism and the ways in which regional analysis can inform them. In Chapter 5 there is a study of the 'Sunbelt v. Frostbelt' debate, characterised in the mid-1970s as 'the second war between the states'. Such rhetoric is examined in relation to the real nature of regional changes taking place. There are also studies of other continuing regional tensions expressed in the East v. West resource issues debate (Chapter 6) and the changing location of poverty within the United States (Chapter 7). Finally, in Chapters 8, 9 and 10, major political attempts to use a regional basis for public policy planning are examined to assess whether the bases of regional analysis and regionalism can be applied as major approaches to social transformation in the late twentieth century. The concluding Chapter 11 attempts to bring together a number of these strands in terms of a theoretical framework and of setting an agenda for studies of regions and regionalism in other nations.

2. The Elements of Regional Differences in the United States

2.1 INTRODUCTION

Regional differences at a particular point in time are essentially a matter of variations in the distributions of particular characteristics. The recognition of such variations may be a matter of perception by the people who live in a region or by those outside the region, or it may be possible to draw boundaries around areas which are seen as having (or not having) particular qualities. In this chapter some of the basic geographical variations within the United States are described and their significance discussed.

2.2 THE USA – A NATION OF GEOGRAPHICAL VARIETY

A most important aspect of America is the variety of people and places contained within the world's fourth largest nation. This variety has played a major part in the nation's economic growth and well-being. It has made it possible to produce a wide range of natural resources, farm products and recreational environments, and so to lay the foundations of affluent self-sufficiency which made the US the leader among the world's nations by the middle of the twentieth century.

Within the borders of the US lie the massive coal reserves of the Appalachian plateaux, and the oil and gas deposits of the margins of the western cordilleras. There are also some of the world's largest gold, silver, copper, iron and other metallic mineral deposits (while some of those in shorter supply in the US occur close by in Canada). The hardwood forests of the eastern states and the massive redwoods and firs of the north-western coasts were without parallel in other temperate nations. The Midwest combination of extensive plains, first-class soils and a climate which is ideal for crops such as corn and soybeans (even though it is dreadful for human beings), has provided a natural basis for the world's most productive farming region. The variety of climates allows the US to produce a range of temperate and subtropical crops for food and industry.

During the period when the distribution of people was related closely to the availability of jobs, and those in turn to raw materials such as coal and iron ore, most people congregated in the north-eastern corner of the US, where timber, coal and iron ore were available, together with access to the city-ports of the north-eastern seaboard with their markets, trade links and accumulations of capital. However, since the development of cheap electricity transmission, together with greater personal mobility and widespread easy communications, in the mid twentieth century, people have been able to choose to live in what they identify as more attractive residential environments, such as Florida, Arizona, California or the 'ecotopia' of Oregon and Washington, and still feel that they can be at the heart of new developments and opportunities. The regional images of people and landscape are thus also integral to an understanding of the changing place of the United States in the wider world.

2.3 VARIATIONS IN NATURAL RESOURCES

The natural features of the US provide striking contrasts of mountain and plain, desert and forest, and have played an important role in defining the geographical regions of the country. In the regional geographies written in the first half of this century, the distinctive climates, terrains, mineral-wealth differences and variations in natural vegetation were related to major differences in life-style among the inhabitants of the United States.

The climates provide an initial set of natural distinctions, the main one of which is that between the humid east and the semi-arid and arid west of the US (Figure 2.1). The eastern half of the

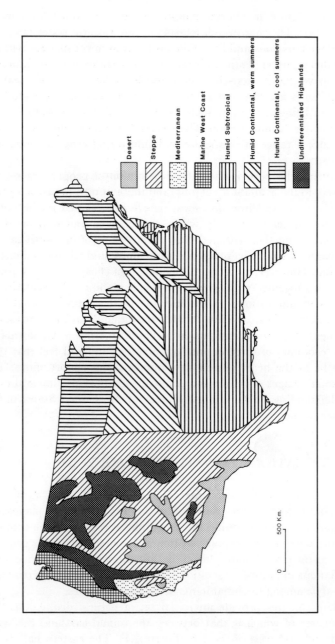

US has plentiful rain throughout the year – sufficient for the riverflow to be maintained with a minimum of variation. To the west of the Mississippi river there is less and less rain, leading to the hot desert conditions of the extreme south-west. In the US west of the Mississippi it is only on the extreme north-western coasts that there is sufficient rainfall to nourish a luxuriant forest cover. The high mountain ranges of western USA attract winter snow which provides soil moisture when it melts in the spring, and leads to rapid runoff amounting to half the annual flows of streams in the space of a week or so. There is a temperature gradient from south to north of the nation, so that the southernmost tip of Florida is seldom troubled by frost in winter, while the northern parts of the Great Lakes area, the Rockies and New England have three months of such conditions with snow lying for long periods each year. Most parts of the US, except the north-west, also have long periods with summer temperatures in the 80s Fahrenheit: it is the length of the summer, rather than its intensity, which varies from south to north. Some regions are more troubled by the most violent forms of weather than others: the climate of Florida and the Gulf coasts is often affected by hurricanes in late summer, while tornados affect the central lowlands in spring.

The terrains of the US are dominated by ranges of mountains along the eastern and western margins, and by a broad central lowland drained by the Mississippi and its tributaries (Figure 2.2). In the east the Appalachian chain has an orientation from south-west to north-east, leaving room for an Atlantic coastal plain which narrows northwards until it gets pinched out altogether at New York. The 400 km width of the Appalachians was a major barrier to movement in colonial times, even though its highest points only rise to just over 2000 m above sea level and in many parts they scarcely exceed 1000 m. Today surface routes are channelled through a restricted number of places. The vast central plain between the Appalachians and Rockies, over 2000 km wide, provides one of the most extensive regions of low-lying, well-drained land in temperate latitudes. The Rockies rise above, and to

FIGURE 2.1 Climatic regions of the US (after Köppen, Trewartha). This classification emphasises the differences between the humid east and arid west

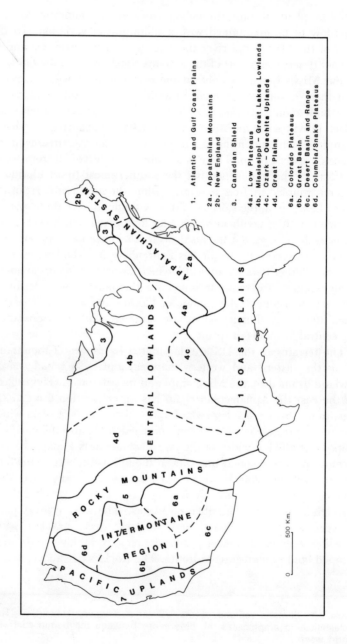

the west of, these central lowlands, and form a discontinuous chain of ranges and peaks from the Canadian border into New Mexico. To their west is a mixture of high plateaux and mountain ranges, split open by deep gorges, and then the ranges and more limited lowland areas which border the Pacific.

The climatic and terrain conditions are basic, and their interaction produced a set of natural regions characterised by distinctive soils and natural vegetation: little of the natural vegetation remains today, but the soils still reflect some of the factors which were important in the past history of ecosystem development. The humid east of the US was covered with mainly hardwood, deciduous woodland, which contained a much greater variety of species than occurs in similar temperate woodlands in Europe. The highest ranges of Appalachia, and the poor, sandy soils of the Atlantic and Gulf coastal plains, tended to be the province of firs and pines in exception to this general rule.

Such dominantly deciduous woodland, and the accompanying recycling of nutrients, was associated with well-developed soils characterised by a good structure, clay-humus basis and nutrient content (alfisols), and these proved among the most fertile soils when lowland areas were cleared of woodland. Places where steeper slopes, or gravel soils, provided more difficult conditions for soil development were most common in the Appalachian uplands. In the cooler far north-east, and along the Canadian border as far as the western end of the Great Lakes, the pines and firs on thin sandy and gravelly parent materials dumped by former ice sheets have produced ashy-grey podzols (spodosols), which have few nutrients and little clay-humus.

With increasing aridity west of the Mississippi, the woodland vegetation gave way to the prairie grasses, and the underlying soils became black and soft with high levels of nutrients (mollisols): these have proved to be the most fertile of all soils for growing grain crops, and dominate the western half of the Midwest and the plains leading up to the Rockies. The Rockies and beyond are mostly too

FIGURE 2.2   The major relief regions of the US (after Fenneman). The most significant feature is the north–south orientation of the major mountain ranges and the central lowlands

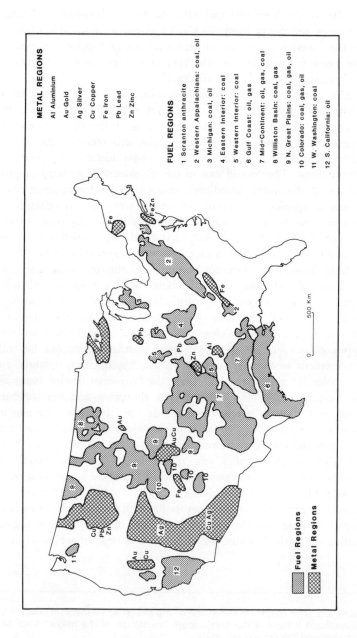

METAL REGIONS

Al Aluminium
Au Gold
Ag Silver
Cu Copper
Fe Iron
Pb Lead
Zn Zinc

FUEL REGIONS

1 Scranton anthracite
2 Western Appalachians: coal, oil
3 Michigan: coal, oil
4 Eastern Interior: coal
5 Western Interior: coal
6 Gulf Coast: oil, gas
7 Mid–Continent: oil, gas, coal
8 Williston Basin: coal, gas
9 N. Great Plains: coal, gas, oil
10 Colorado: coal, gas, oil
11 W. Washington: coal
12. S. California: oil

0   500 Km.

Fuel Regions
Metal Regions

arid or too steep for mature soils to develop, but some of the soil materials can provide a good basis for irrigation farming.

The US possesses a great variety of mineral wealth, but this is not evenly distributed, and so contributes to regional strengths and weaknesses (Figure 2.3). The Appalachians have vast stores of coal, particularly in the west-central portion where the plateau is underlain by flat, thick seams of high-quality coal. The same areas also contain moderate deposits of oil and natural gas – the earliest to be exploited commercially in the US. Only small quantities of metallic minerals have been discovered in the eastern US. Such resources are most common in the Rockies and other western cordilleras (gold, silver, lead, zinc, copper) and in the ancient rocks which come to the surface along the shores of Lake Superior (iron ore). Other mineral deposits occur in sedimentary layers, as in the case of the phosphate rock of Florida and the lignite layers of the Great Plains. The salt deposits of Louisiana occur in subsurface dome-shaped masses. Oil and natural gas occur in the greatest quantities along the margins of the western mountain ranges, stretching from Texas and California northwards to Alaska, and in coastal and offshore deposits along the Gulf coast. Energy-poor regions (such as New England), and energy-rich regions (such as the Gulf from Texas to western Florida) can be identified on the basis of the distributions of coal, oil and gas resources.

The distribution of these natural resources provides the basis of many regional characteristics, but it is the human usage of regions which determines their ultimate character. It is not enough to possess natural wealth: human usage may, or may not, result in the extraction of that wealth; people may either use it carefully over as long a period as possible, or may remove it rapidly; and the resources may be used or processed locally (thus returning the wealth created to the place where it is extracted), or may be taken elsewhere. Much of Appalachia could have been rich today if the wealth extracted from its coal mines and forests had been used locally, but the companies which cut the timber and coal took it to

---

FIGURE 2.3   Mineral resource regions of the US (after Watson 1982). Not only are there distinct fuel and metal regions, but also coal and oil/gas regions. There are also major parts of the country without mineral resources

be used in manufacturing industry based in cities outside the mountains. The profits have been mainly used to pay shareholders in those cities. The producing region has remained poor. The coasts and swamplands of southern Florida, the deserts of Arizona, and the isolated valleys of Appalachia remained ignored and of low value until new demands for amenity and recreation recognised a new set of resource values in the local natural environment. Then these places experienced rapid population growth.

2.4 VARIATIONS AMONG PEOPLE

The history of the occupation of the North American continent by human beings superimposed new characteristics on the natural diversity of regional patterns. There has been an increasing intensity of occupation of the land which has also imposed further changes. The fact that regions distinguished on the basis of human activities have been less permanent than those which have arisen from the interaction of natural forces has tempted too many authors of geography texts to base their regional divisions on the more permanent physical features, or to use a mixed basis of human and natural features.

The peoples of the United States today have a wide range of origins and distributions, and this variety provides a major element of regional distinctiveness. Phases of immigration and internal migration have produced constantly changing patterns of peoples and their cultural impact on the landscapes. The pre-European inhabitants had distinctive regional patterns of distribution related to natural conditions, but the greatest changes and shifts of emphasis have occurred since the arrival of European colonists from the fifteenth century. Not only did different European nationalities come with different intentions and customs – Spanish, French and British – but even within the British contingents there were contrasts between the aristocratic southern tidewater plantation owners, the puritans in New England and the enterprising family farmers who settled much of the Middle Atlantic. These cultural characteristics have left their mark on regions today.

Black slaves were introduced to the southern tidewater colonies after 1619 and, following independence in 1776, the amerinds were largely removed from their tribal lands to new reservations in the

West. The South became the land of the aristocratic white, some poor whites and lots of black slaves, and this mixture of peoples and distinctive culture was responsible for a distinctive regional identity which affects the present geography. The work ethic and commercial appetite of the New England Yankees is associated with trading enterprise around the world and with the early development of factory industries – attitudes which were at least partly passed on to settlers who moved from New England to the Midwest. The Hispanic presence in the south-west, together with a concentration of the remnant of amerinds in that region, has also been instrumental in imparting a special sense of region, which has remained despite a major influx of new settlers from the Midwest during the twentieth century (Michener, 1985).

However, these population characteristics have become modified by internal migrations, and by immigration from abroad, in the twentieth century. Groups from eastern and southern Europe have altered the ethnic maps of many of the major northern cities in particular. Large numbers of black people moved from the poverty-stricken rural South to the centres of urban population in the north-east and west coast (but few to the far north-west). Hispanic groups have become prominent in the New York, Chicago and Miami areas, and Asians on the Pacific coast. It is likely that this process of diffusion and inter-mixture will continue, so that proportions of many minority groups become less distinctively associated with particular regions.

The present pattern of regional differences is also a result of past changes and trends in economic and social conditions. These have given rise to, firstly, a set of variations in economic opportunity. Much of the nation's wealth is still created in the older cities of the north-east, and especially in the 'Megalopolis' corridor stretching from Boston through New York, Philadelphia and Baltimore to Washington DC (sometimes known as 'Boswash', or 'Bosnywash'). Incomes are higher, and there is a greater concentration of the 'control centres' of business and government in this region, than in any other in the US: this is still the core of the nation. This core may be extended westwards through the 'Manufacturing Belt' to Chicago. Despite its most recent history of depressed manufacturing production, this region is still generating many new jobs in service industries. Another core of economic and political power has developed since 1950 in the far south-west around Los Angeles and

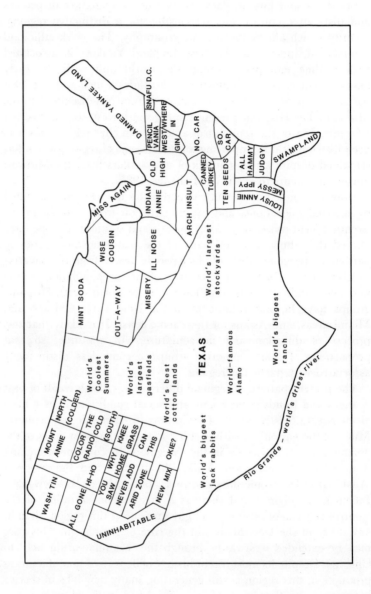

San Francisco – the goal for so many moving out of the traditional concentrations of people in the north-east. There may also be another high density of urban-industrial functions, economic growth and population emerging in the south-east from Florida through Atlanta and along the Gulf coast to Houston. The definitions of such cores may vary, but large complexes of metropolitan development continue to be associated with the greatest choices of job opportunities.

In between these 'cores' are various sorts of 'peripheries': most of them are rural in character, such as the Appalachian region, the Great Plains, the rural south, the northern mountains and some of the western arid plateaux. Such regions were discovered to be lagging behind the affluence of the rest of the nation in the early 1960s, and efforts were made by the US government in that decade to even out the inequities. In the 1970s these regions often discovered that they also had attractions for many by virtue of their isolation and access to recreational amenities, and so the peripheral context had some positive advantages. House (1983) compiled a list of regional types within the United States based on characteristics of economic growth and/or decline in relation to the national cores and peripheries.

Social differences have emerged between groups within the US, and have affected the range of choice available for residential location decisions. If you are black and live in central Boston, you do not have much choice: the scope of social and economic space is limited to a few blocks for all but a small group. However, if you are a white executive, all sorts of attractions and possibilities will be open, depending on whether your priorities dictate a place near your favourite occupation of coastal fishing, golfing or congregating with like minds (and incomes).

The recent trend towards an emphasis on residential location close to amenity rather than to workplace has become important in the move to rural places in the 1970s. This has meant that middle-class life-styles based on urban, white-collar employment have taken over many of the rural districts in contact with metropolitan centres.

FIGURE 2.4   A Texan's perception of the rest of the United States (compiled from several postcard versions)

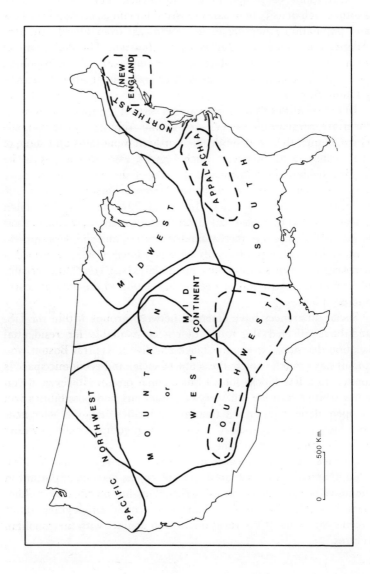

2.5 PERCEPTIONS OF REGIONAL VARIATIONS

Regional variations have been perceived in various ways by those in different parts of the US (Gould and White, 1986). Such perceptions have been portrayed in the New Yorker's, or the Texan's view of the rest of their country (Figure 2.4). They have given rise to the stereotypes of the sharp Yankee businessman, the gentlemanly but not very practical southerner, or the Texan with the largest or everything.

Other attempts to establish the level of identification of local people with regional labels include the study by Cox (1972) of the perceptions of his geography students at Ohio State University (Figure 2.5). Some parts of the United States were clearly related to a particular regional title, and their boundaries were consistently placed. A study by Zelinsky (1980) was based on the vernacular use of regional titles by companies listed in the Yellow Pages of the telephone companies. This produced some surprises: for instance, the term 'Appalachia' was used much less than might be expected. This can be explained by the fact that many of those living in Appalachia see the term as a rude word – implying that one lives in a shack and cannot afford shoes for the children. Companies listed in the Yellow Pages tend to choose names with a positive image.

Zelinsky previously (1973) based a regional division of the principal cultural areas of the United States on language, religion and politics. While 90 per cent of Americans speak English, there are concentrations of Spanish-speaking peoples in the south-west and southern Florida; of Chinese in west-coast cities; and of Indian and other aboriginal languages on the reservations and in Alaska. Two-thirds of Americans profess a Protestant affiliation, and these form large majorities in the South and Midwest. Roman Catholics are in the highest proportions in the south-west and in the large cities of the North. Political loyalties have tended to change in recent years, and this will be discussed further in Chapter 5.

FIGURE 2.5 Ohio student perceptions of the regions of the United States (after Cox, 1972)

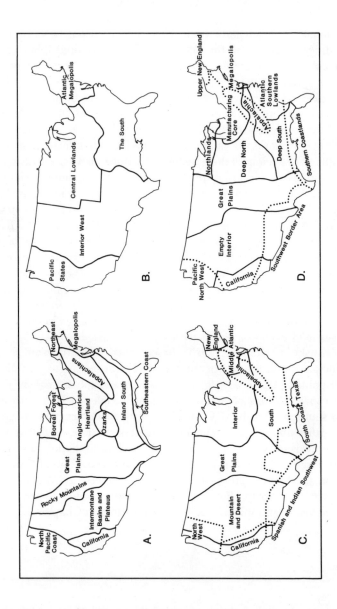

2.6 VARIATIONS IN REGIONAL DEFINITIONS

Most regional divisions are devised for a particular purpose. The geographer may wish to use regional divisions as a basis for describing the differences between parts of a country in physical or economic terms; the federal agency or major corporation may use them for dividing up the territory of the nation for easy administration of programmes or sales forces; and individuals may divide the nation into what may be defined as 'attractive' or 'unattractive' places to live. At present it is clear that many Americans view Florida and the West (especially the Denver area and California) as the most attractive places, since they move there in great numbers when free to do so.

It is instructive to compare the regional divisions of the United States which have formed the basis of geographical accounts of the country in the late 1970s and early 1980s (Paterson, 1984; Birdsall and Florin, 1978; Starkey, Robinson and Miller, 1975; White, Foscue and McKnight, 1979). There is little more than general agreement on the names of regions and their boundaries (Figure 2.6). The names of the regions and the boundaries used by each author, or group of authors, reflect a variety of bases used for a single regional division. None of these divisions is made on the consistent basis of a single factor – economic, physical, single state and urban characteristics are mixed. These maps demonstrate the difficulties which accompany a purely descriptive approach, but may also indicate something of deeper significance: perhaps the confusion is generated by the fact that most regional geographies of this type assume a 'snapshot' static view of regional divisions. A historical input is required to help unravel the complexity.

Further disagreement over regional boundaries is encountered when the regions used by Federal government agencies are compared. It might be expected that there would be some co-ordination at this level, but the Bureau of Census identifies one set of regions and the Federal Reserve Board another, and this

---

FIGURE 2.6   A comparison of four regional divisions of the US as suggested by the authors of regional geography texts: (A) White, Foscue and McKnight (1979); (B) Starkey, Robinson and Miller (1975); (C) Paterson (1984); (D) Birdsall and Florin (1978)

continues through many of the agencies. The Bureau of Economic Analysis within the Department of Commerce has identified a set of Economic Areas which are much smaller, and relate to a local spatial level within the larger regions.

2.7 REGIONS AND INTERNAL POLITICAL DIVISIONS

Of all the different bases used in recent regional geographies of the United States, none use the political boundaries of the states, or other political division. Many of the state boundaries 'owe more to geometry than geography' (Paterson, 1982), especially in the western half of the United States, but it has to be recognised that many important decisions are taken within those boundaries. Decisions over land use, natural resource usage and many commercial activities and services (education in particular) are made by each state, and may be very different from those in adjacent states. The state is the key element in allowing local opinion to be expressed and to be involved in such decisions. Although it has been said that the states are 'artificial units' from a geographical point of view (Paterson, 1982), this statement is based on a 'geography' which is linked to natural features. Suggestions that the states provide an uneven division of the natural territory which should be tidied up are unlikely to bear fruit. The established pattern of state boundaries is not going to be changed, but will remain an important factor in the way in which local geographies change. If the internal differentiation of human activities at the regional scale within the US becomes a matter of public policy, the boundaries of groups of states may be the most appropriate for regional divisions.

2.8 CONCLUSIONS

From this discussion of the nature of regions in the United States it is clear that there is no agreement on a set of accepted regional divisions within the nation's borders. If there were a set accepted by various levels of government and business for administrative purposes, and by geographers for purposes of description and analysis, this book would take a different approach.

The present confusion and complexity is partly because the geographical regions have resulted from a complex interaction of processes: the natural environment, cultural backgrounds of people, economic-political systems in force and the impact of changing technologies have produced in different combinations a set of regions which defy precise and consistent definition. This confusion can be untangled to an extent by taking a historical view of the evolution of the regional geography of the United States.

3. The Historic Basis of Present Regional Differences in the United States

3.1 INTRODUCTION

Although regional differences in the United States can be based on natural environmental distinctions between the parts of the nation, or even on the sales territories established by a firm, such divisions can never be all-embracing or for all time. The sheer complexity of American geography today requires not just a survey of current variations in landscape and life, but an investigation of the contributions of past events and societies. The most helpful approach for creating the fullest understanding of these differences is through an evolutionary historical context. This makes it possible to untangle some of the factors contributing to regional differences, and to understand the ways in which they have changed over time and resulted in the differential accumulation of distinctive landscapes and ways of life in particular parts of the US.

The pattern adopted in this chapter is based on a summary framework for six major phases of American history (Figure 3.1). This framework includes comments for each phase on the social-economic system, its relationship with the natural environment, the level of mobility available, the type of settlements which were typical, and the political system of the time. These factors are related to the specific types of regional conditions which accounted for the major geographical differences within the territory of the present US at each phase.

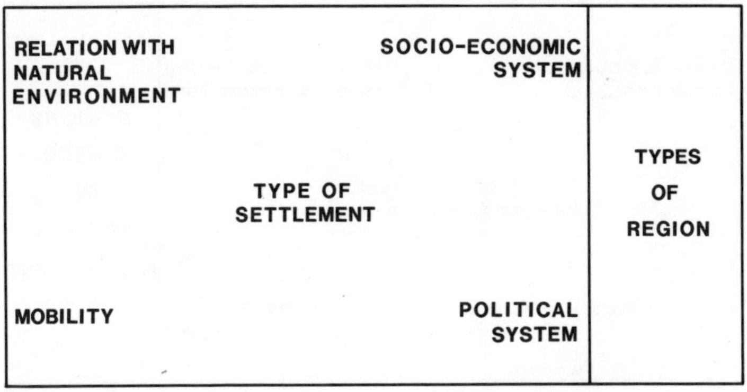

FIGURE 3.1   A framework for historical regional analysis

3.2 REGIONS BEFORE COLUMBUS

The arrival of Europeans in North America resulted in the first group of major changes in the processes which gave rise to distinctive regional perceptions. Up to the late fifteenth century the continent was occupied by relatively small numbers of people living in tribal groups and dependent on the natural environment rather than on their own capacity to produce a surplus of food for their needs. Then European peoples from different national backgrounds, and with different objectives and perceptions of the new continent, began the series of changes which have resulted in the present geography of the USA.

The aboriginal inhabitants of North America may be divided into groups of cultures, each of which reflected their dependence on the local availability of natural resources (Figure 3.2). The extremes of humid/arid, heat and cold were clearly reflected in ways of life. The population density which could be supported by the natural environment determined not only diet and annual cycle of tasks, but also the level of culture which developed.

In the eastern portion of what is now the USA, the dominant humid conditions and forest cover gave rise to a variety of ecological niches for animals to be hunted, plentiful river fish, and good soils for agriculture. The amerind tribes who inhabited this territory lived in permanent villages of several thousand people, and cleared patches of the forest for cultivating corn, beans and squashes. Some

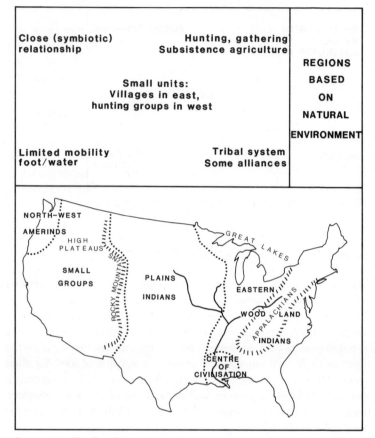

FIGURE 3.2   The Pre-Columban regional geography of the present US

of the tribes made treaties with each other, and maintained peace over long periods. Those tribes with coastal locations along the Atlantic were often smaller and less influential than the inland groups (Michener, 1978).

The southernmost of these eastern woodland tribes achieved a major technological revolution just before Europeans reached their continent, and the evidence which remains of these events in the southern Mississippi valley points to the emergence of a civilisation based on surplus production of food. Their remnants, identified in the Cherokees, Chickasaws and Choctaws, possessed a range of technical skills including pottery, textiles and medicines, and many of their farming methods were at least the equivalent of those used in Europe at the time.

West of the Mississippi, the amerinds were organised differently. The climate was subhumid and supported only grassland. Whereas the eastern woodland amerinds had a variety of materials at their command for clothing, utensils and construction, the prairie amerind made use of the bison for food, clothing, tipi fabric and most utensils. The bison, which grazed the grasslands of the prairies and high plains, were for long chased on foot by hunting groups (200–300 people, with tribes being split and perhaps gathering only once a year). This occurred until horses released by early Spanish settlers became available in the sixteenth century. Some tribes on the woodland-prairie margins combined cultivation with seasonal hunting forays, but others were totally dependent on moving with the herds of bison. The grassland may have been extended eastwards by the annual practice of firing the grass in order to encourage higher densities of the food-producing animals on which these amerinds depended. Densities of population must have been much lower than in the eastern woodlands owing to the extensive areas over which the bison grazed.

Farther west again the resources available became more sparse as aridity increased, and the family unit became the dominant social group. The amerinds here hunted animals and collected from local plants. Some groups in the extreme south-west managed primitive irrigation, or gathered in cliff-dwellings, but total numbers were very small.

In the far north-west of the present USA the high rainfall of the Pacific coastlands (extending northwards into southern Alaska) permitted another distinctive life-style. The amerinds here lived in the forests of massive Douglas Fir trees and along streams teeming with salmon. Although few in total numbers, they dwelt in well-organised villages and in homes built of wooden planks. They ventured to sea in boats hollowed out of tree trunks which were large enough to take up to 30 people, who would attack whales. Their religion is symbolised in the totem poles which they carved and set up in and around the villages.

Alaska was inhabited by a variety of aboriginal peoples in addition to the amerinds along the southern coast. The nunumiats (eskimos) migrated into North America after the amerinds, and were concentrated along the eastern and northern coasts of Alaska. Their natural resources were mainly obtained from the sea due to the low productivity of land environments, and settlement was concentrated along the coasts. Some inland hunting of caribou was carried out by groups in the late summer when the animals were at their fattest. On the far western islands the aleuts were the last to cross from Asia, and had a distinctive life based on fishing and the hunting of seals.

Little contact seems to have taken place between these different groups of people due to a low level of personal mobility, and many were cut off from each other by expanses of desert or by mountain ranges. Contact with other groups did occur around the margins of tribal territories, but usually within the natural/cultural regions. Their different cultures were thus maintained on a regional basis which was closely related to the distribution of natural resources. Since their technology was scarcely beyond that of the Stone Age, they had little impact on the natural environment outside the woodland clearings in the humid east and the relatively minor extensions of the prairie grasslands due to burning. The relatively small groups of people were governed by strict and slowly changing social taboos evolving over centuries. They lived in harmony with their natural environment and saw themselves as part of it. Only a few relics, such as settlement mounds and middens, together with the lines of old amerind trails taken by modern routes, have been passed to subsequent cultural landscapes.

3.3 EARLY EUROPEAN SETTLERS

Within 200 years of the first arrival of Europeans in North America a new regional pattern had been imposed. Peoples from different parts of Europe brought with them their own traditions of farming, building and social organisation (Stilgoe, 1982). Most of them were searching for a source of immediate wealth to take back to Europe, but some came intending to stay and create a new type of society. All had concepts of land ownership and society which were very different from those of the aboriginal peoples. The Europeans brought with them medieval concepts of 'wilderness' (unsettled land fraught with hidden and dark dangers), and the virtues of reclaiming this land and its peoples for civilised settlement.

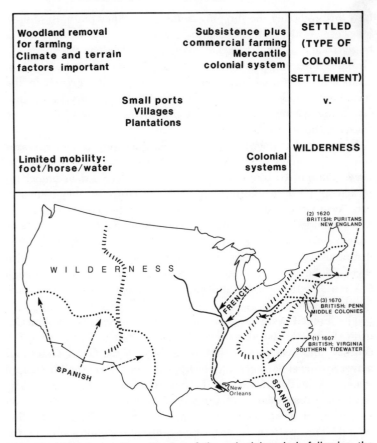

FIGURE 3.3 The regional geography of the colonial period: following the 1763 defeat of the French, British territory extended to the Mississippi

The Spaniards were the first to settle parts of the continent (Figure 3.3), beginning soon after the 1492 crossing of the Atlantic by Columbus and rapidly followed by other opportunists looking for sources of gold to enhance their home estates. They were the first of a series of European venturers due to the enterprise of Columbus and the ambition of their monarchs, and began by exploring the Caribbean area. During the early part of the sixteenth century they sent groups into Florida and south-eastern USA, but found no gold. They retained only Florida because it provided a base for protecting the shipping route home. They put most of their long-term settlement efforts into New Spain (now Mexico) and a buffer zone to the north of that colony, initially along the upper Rio Grande. This buffer zone was extended into a new province of Tejas when a threat appeared to come from the French in the Mississippi valley in the early eighteenth century, and into California when the Russians began to move down the Pacific coasts in the late eighteenth century.

It may be that the Spaniards were most at home in the semi-arid south-west which was akin to their home environment, and this view is supported by the fact that they transferred their homeland settlement patterns and farming methods. However, they were also very keen on guarding the silver-producing centres in Mexico. It was concluded after a number of expeditions that there was little or no gold or silver farther north. Much of south-western USA is distinguished by the relics of these former Spanish settlements with their adobe buildings and patterns of land-holding, although modern American styles and landscapes have now replaced them to a large extent.

The French were next on the scene, entering North America from the north-east along the St Lawrence river in the sixteenth century, and eventually penetrating through the Great Lakes and across low-level portages into the upper tributaries of the Mississippi system. A marked feature of French settlement which has left its mark on subsequent land use is the long-lot division, based on narrow river frontages for the plots and strips of land extending inland. This pattern is still significant in the landscapes of the Mississippi delta and the layout of the city of New Orleans. Most of the French influence was concentrated in the Canadian province of Québec, but there are relics in the US around Detroit, St Louis and New Orleans.

The British colonists left the greatest marks on the present regional geography of the US, but were much later in arriving. Although some of the British sea captains, such as Sir Walter Raleigh, attempted to establish permanent settlements on the largely unoccupied Atlantic coast in the late sixteenth century, the fuller occupation of these territories had to await the death of Elizabeth I in 1603 and the signing of a peace treaty between England and Spain. As soon as this was achieved, two companies were set up in London and Plymouth, and given royal charters to explore and settle the lands between Spanish Florida and the French St Lawrence. The London Company was allotted the southern coasts, and the Plymouth Company the northern, but there was a section in the middle where they overlapped, between the Hudson and Chesapeake estuaries. Settlement of the overlapping zone was to be left until the northern and southern areas were filled with people. This division between the two companies was perhaps the single most significant factor in the subsequent internal differentiation of the United States: this was a matter of almost arbitrary decision-making in England, and was not related to natural resources.

The Plymouth Company did not have much success in establishing groups of settlers along the northern coasts, and it was the London Company which set up the first permanent settlement at Jamestown on the Western shore of Chesapeake Bay in 1607. After some early problems it was discovered that tobacco would grow well in these southern colonies with their long, hot summers. The tidewater allowed the small ships of the day to berth at small private quays at each plantation. There was no need for more central port cities. In the 1620s the Crown took over part of this area as the colony of Virginia, and Maryland was established in 1630. By the end of the seventeenth century similar plantations, using white-indentured and black-slave labour, occupied the southern coastlands of the Carolinas and Georgia to the Florida border and produced indigo, sugar cane and rice in addition to the tobacco. A distinctive 'southern' society emerged based on English aristocratic practices, commercial products which could be marketed in England, and on individual plantations rather than larger settlements.

In 1620 the Pilgrim Fathers landed by mistake in what became New England. They had to obtain the correct papers from the almost defunct Plymouth Company, and then produced a very different society from that which was developing in the southern tidewater areas. The puritan groups which began to head for the Massachusetts Bay colony in increasing numbers had a religious, rather than commercial, perception of their purpose in establishing a colony, and at first the prospects of creating a new type of society were paramount. Settlement took place in compact villages, or townships, and each community was subject to internal control: in each township a small group of proprietors was entrusted with the responsibility for extending the settled area and for watching over the religious education of the population. By the late seventeenth century this initial enthusiasm had given way to more basic economic goals, and to more democratic local government, but another distinctive geographical pattern had been established. It is still evident in the township divisions of Boston and the rest of New England.

The limited ability of both companies to attract and finance colonies in the new lands meant that the zone of overlap in the Middle Atlantic coast, which was designated to be filled after the exclusive zones, appeared open to others in the early seventeenth century. Groups of Swedes and Dutch established settlements on the lower Delaware and Hudson rivers: those of the Swedes were short-lived and taken over by the Dutch, who were in turn removed in the 1660s when the British marched into the main settlement of New Amsterdam and renamed it New York. This was the signal for rapid occupation of land by British and other European settlers who had been deterred by the aristocratic control of the south or the puritan discrimination in the north. William Penn obtained much of the Middle Atlantic land from the Duke of York in payment of debts, and opened the new colony of Pennsylvania to those who would wish to settle and develop the land without too much antagonism towards the amerinds. This open policy coincided with an increase in the size of ships plying the Atlantic in the early eighteenth century, and also with the exodus of Germans from Central Europe and of 'Scotch-Irish' from northern Ireland. Penn's capital of Philadelphia became the largest American city by the mid eighteenth century, while New York also grew rapidly as a port and banking centre. The settlement of the Middle Atlantic was more akin to that in New England than that in the southern colonies, since it was based on family-unit farms without a major export crop. However, farming in the Middle Atlantic became more profitable than that in New England due to better soils, and by the mid eighteenth century this section was producing wheat for export to other colonies in America and the West Indies.

In this way the North–South distinction within the US was instigated. The North was characterised by coastal port cities, family farms in the immediate hinterlands of market towns, and a frontier zone stretching into the Appalachian woodlands. Most of the northern people had cut themselves off from their European origins. The South was a land of plantations with their own access to ocean trade routes, and less corporate life developed outside the gatherings of plantation owners. There was much coming and going across the Atlantic, particularly in links between the southern plantations and England.

By the end of the colonial period there was a string of colonies lining the eastern coast, but there had been little penetration of the Appalachian mountains to the west: these mountains, and the lands beyond, were regarded as 'wilderness'. The conflict with French settlers and traders to the north was resolved in 1763 after a series of minor wars, and it appeared that the British colonies could now expand westwards in peace. In the early 1770s, however, the British government succeeded in uniting some very diverse groups of colonists against it by a series of ill-judged measures, and in 1783, after seven years of revolutionary war following the 1776 Declaration of Independence, the new nation of the United States of America came into being.

Throughout this period movement within the colonies had been easier than in the pre-Columbus days, but was still very restricted by comparison with later times, except along the waterways. Most contacts were still with the home country, but there was some trade between the West Indian colonies (rum, molasses), the Middle Atlantic wheat farmers and New England (dried fish, ships). The port cities of the middle and northern colonies were the centre for both mercantile and political activities. The latter involved attempts to control the colonies from England and also the development of a movement for independence. It was in these cities that conflicts between the two sets of attitudes came to a head.

Although the major North–South variations were reflected in the different systems of land-use and settlement, the most clear-cut differences at the time were those between the remaining wilderness and the settled areas. At the local scale within the settled colonies there were distinctions between town and country, cultivated valley floors and wooded uplands, riverbank and areas isolated from water transport. It did not take many miles for the landscape to change from commercial port to fields of vegetables, then a belt of woodland, fields of grain crops and cattle-grazing in the edges of the woodland wilderness. The port cities of the north-east coast, the plantations of the south-east, the French long-lots and the Spanish-style settlements of the upper Rio Grande, provide the most 'historical' features of the present US landscape. The longer period of occupation by European cultures, which they reflect, plays an important part in an understanding of the present social structures of these regions.

3.4 INDEPENDENCE AND THE FRONTIER 'WESTS'

The colonial era of early European settlement produced the seeds of regional differences within the new nation created by the Declaration of Independence in 1776. After 1783 these differences were perpetuated in various ways and their influence was spread westwards as new lands were acquired and settled (Figure 3.4). As people migrated into new lands, the 'West' was first located in and just beyond the Appalachians, then moved across the Mississippi by the mid nineteenth century, and to the Pacific coast by the end of the century. The frontier conditions, which were associated with the 'West', were not always a matter of individual families struggling with the amerinds and wilderness. Although settlement of some areas, such as upper New York state, awaited the removal of the amerinds by force, frontier life in the North often consisted of planting new towns, with the accompanying financial speculation which this involved. In the first half of the nineteenth century new settlements were concentrated along the main river arteries.

Commercial farming was necessary from the start to pay off the debts incurred in purchasing land, and there was a westward movement of initial wheat farming followed by mixed farming as far as the climatic conditions allowed (i.e. to just west of the Mississippi). In the southern states cotton took over as the main plantation crop, and provided an economic basis for geographical expansion. New plantations extended westwards around the southern edge of the Appalachians and into the Mississippi valley. A plantation owner in the 1840s might own several plantations: one near the Atlantic coast where few crops were grown, but slaves were bred; one in a place where production was at its peak; and one which was being cleared near the western limits of development. The two major channels of westward movement – across the northern and southern states – perpetuated and enhanced the North–South cultural division.

New lands and new people were basic to this westward

Climate and terrain factors important	Early free market (capitalist) commercial system Primary sector dominant	ESTABLISHED SETTLEMENT v. FRONTIER (WILDERNESS)
	Medium and small towns villages, farms	──────── NORTH
Increasing mobility: Canals, railroads, turnpike roads	Republican system: Federal, state, county system established	v. SOUTH

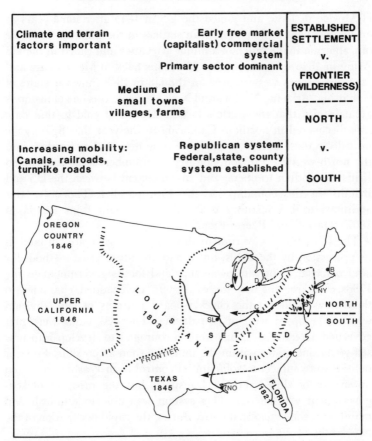

FIGURE 3.4 The regional geography of the US between Independence (1776) and the Civil War (1861). The lands west of the Mississippi were acquired at this time

movement. Within 75 years of independence, the US had acquired almost all its present land area. It began by owning the lands south of the Great Lakes and east of the Mississippi (apart from Florida). The former colonies became the first states, and gave up their claims to lands west of the Appalachians so that those lands could be sold to repay the debts of the Federal government. In 1803 the Louisiana Purchase from France added a broad swathe of land west of the Mississippi, and in 1819 the Spanish government gave up Florida. Texas gained its independence from the new Republic of Mexico in 1836, and joined the US in 1845 after some years as an independent nation. American settlers in the Mexican province of California made much of a minor grievance and called in the US Army in 1846 to chase the few Mexicans back to Mexico City and obtain the south-western area for the US in 1848 (now the states of California, Arizona, Nevada and New Mexico). It is one of history's great ironies that the world's largest deposit of gold to that date was discovered in northern California in the year that Spain gave up title to these lands. At the same time new settlers flooding into the north-western 'Oregon Country' outnumbered the established British-Canadian trappers, and an agreement between the US and Britain set the boundary at the 49th parallel. The only later additions to US territory were Alaska (bought from Russia in 1867), Hawaii and Puerto Rico.

The US Federal government thus had a massive area of land in its possession by the 1840s, but it had already devised methods for land disposal to private ownership and for its government in the 1780s. The rectangular survey system gave added character to these new lands by the checker-board patterns of land division which it adopted west of Appalachia. The new lands were first governed as territories, but were encouraged to develop into new self-governing states within the union as soon as possible. Frontier politics were subject to some initial control from Washington, even in an era of slow overland transport, but the prospect of self-government was offered. This system was able to establish and maintain a single national entity during the rapid occupation of the new lands.

As the tide of settlement moved west, there were inevitable conflicts with the amerind inhabitants, who had a different view of land to the new Americans: as with many tribal societies existing on a subsistence basis, they regarded the ownership of land as a communal matter, whereas the settlers saw it as an individual's right to own land. These opposing perceptions resulted in conflict and, tribe by tribe, the amerinds were displaced from their lands. At first they were moved to large reservations beyond the Mississippi, but in the later nineteenth century even these were demanded by farmers and miners, and so the remnants of the amerind tribes were moved to smaller reservations, mainly in unwanted arid areas. Their populations were decimated by European diseases, warfare and the hardships of removal to difficult lands where the environmental conditions clashed with their slowly evolved cultures.

The availability of so much land at relatively low prices, together with improved means of transport and information about the new lands, led to increases in the numbers of immigrants attracted from Europe. The southern states continued to recruit mainly from Britain, and particularly England, but also added to the black slave population. Up to 1808 the black population increase was still partly by the international slave trade, but after that date it was by natural increase. Natural increase had been significant in the growth of the black population in North America from the seventeenth century (and can be compared to the natural decreases in the black populations of the Caribbean). In the growing cities and farming areas of the northern US, immigrants from Germany, Ireland and Scandinavia gathered increasingly from 1820, and produced a mosaic of ethnic communities by the mid nineteenth century.

As the lands were obtained, and more and more new people arrived, transport technology provided improved means of movement across the huge distances to the westward-moving frontier. Up to 1825 rivers remained the main avenues for transport to the interior: farmers in Ohio had to ship their produce down the Mississippi, through New Orleans and up the east coast to the main city markets on the north-east coast. There were some local turnpike roads in the more heavily populated parts of the Middle Atlantic states in particular, but mostly in short, unconnected lengths. In 1825 the Erie Canal was opened and at once became a major routeway connecting the interior with New York – already the main port and largest city in the US. In 1830 the first railroad was opened for a few miles out of Baltimore, and these two modes of transport, canal and railroad, took up an increasing proportion of capital investment to the 1850s, by which time the major east coast cities were linked to Chicago and the Mississippi. These links were stimulated by competition between the states on the northern and middle Atlantic coasts, each of which attempted to gain control of the growing internal trade by the construction of rail and/or canal links. Development was slower in the South, since most capital was still being invested in slaves.

The North–South differences came to a head in the 1850s, since almost all the new territories which had been added in the 1840s were in the North. They would have a non-slave clause in their constitutions when accepted as states. Measures to open up new lands freely to settlers, and to build railroads to the west coast, were held up by the maintenance of an even representation in the US Senate from the northern and southern states, and by suspicions of each other's motives. When Abraham Lincoln was elected as president of the US in 1861, the people of the South realised that further pressures would be placed on them and decided to secede from the Union and establish themselves as a separate nation. The rest of the US would not allow this, and the Civil War ensued.

This period of development was thus characterised by the formalisation of the North v. South regional contrasts as the westward movements of people in both regions took their established cultures with them. The improved transport technology gradually changed the scale of human economic and social space. Products were exchanged between the new farming areas of the interior lowlands and the early factories of New England and the Middle Atlantic cities. This changing scale of mobility is reflected in the relative sizes of the county divisions established at this time in the eastern and mid-western parts of the nation. Since the county town was ideally a place within a day's travel from home, the initial county divisions were often very small – ten miles or so from one side of the county to the other was common. This period also introduced other new features to the regional mosaic – inland towns which were generally river ports, and grid-like field patterns.

3.5 THE CIVIL WAR AND ITS AFTERMATH: THE LATE NINETEENTH AND EARLY TWENTIETH CENTURY

The Civil War ended in 1865, but it marked a watershed between distinctive sets of processes producing regional differences inside the US (Figure 3.5). After the war the South became an exploited region, and descended into a poverty which differentiated it from the rest of the US for 100 years. The 'Far West' was differentiated in people's minds from the 'Midwest', and became the location for new types of development, beginning with a succession of mining enterprises and then followed by irrigation farming after the turn of the century. The North, however, consolidated its role as the centre

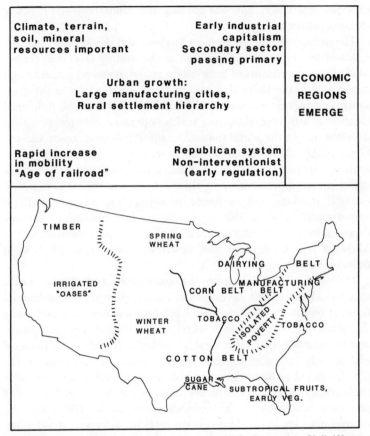

Climate, terrain,
soil, mineral
resources important

Early industrial
capitalism
Secondary sector
passing primary

ECONOMIC

Urban growth:
Large manufacturing cities,
Rural settlement hierarchy

REGIONS

EMERGE

Rapid increase
in mobility
"Age of railroad"

Republican system
Non-interventionist
(early regulation)

TIMBER

SPRING
WHEAT

DAIRYING   BELT

IRRIGATED
"OASES"

MANUFACTURING
BELT

CORN BELT

TOBACCO

WINTER
WHEAT

ISOLATED
POVERTY   TOBACCO

COTTON BELT

SUGAR
CANE   SUBTROPICAL FRUITS,
EARLY VEG.

FIGURE 3.5 The regional geography of the US, from the Civil War to
approximately 1920

of national economic and social life, with the urbanising Atlantic
seaboard forming the core of a major 'Manufacturing Belt' which
eventually stretched inland to the Great Lakes and linked with the
world's most productive farming region in the Midwest. The North-
South cultural differences gave way to a new economic distinction.
The South was an ignored, undeveloped and exploited region, in
which defensive social structures became entrenched. The North's
social and economic openness, combined with high levels of
productivity in farming and manufacturing, resulted in the US
becoming the world's wealthiest nation. The Far West was at an

experimental stage, but was gaining the reputation of providing exciting prospects for the future.

The north-east, including New England and the Middle Atlantic, retained and enhanced its position as the leading economic centre. Manufacturing continued to be concentrated in this region, although it was only in the 1870s that coal replaced water power as the main source of energy for industry. This led to a shift of industrial location at a time of increasing scale of operation and technological development in the metal industries: the Pittsburgh region and the Great Lake shores became the new centres of manufacturing growth. The ports of New York, Boston, Baltimore and Philadelphia still dominated overseas trade, since Europe was the main source of external markets and exchange products. The rapid growth of urban populations in this region in the late nineteenth century exposed its relative lack of farmland, and food produced in the Midwest was brought in and much was also exported through these east coast ports.

The market demands from east coast cities and abroad meant that the Midwest had developed as a distinctive set of commercial farming regions by the late nineteenth century: the dairy belt along the north, the corn belt with its related cattle and hog production, and the wheat belts farther west, extended over millions of hectares and already produced much more than could be consumed in the US. Gluts led to low prices and poor farmers and, since they were the nation's largest constituency, almost led to the election of a president belonging to the farmer's party in the 1890s. On the eastern margins of the Midwest the steel industry was developing, based on Pennsylvania coking coal and iron ore mined around the Great Lakes. In addition, the processing of farm produce, and the production of implements and machinery, were leading to a greater diversity of manufacturing, concentrated in former route nodes such as Cincinnati, Cleveland and Chicago. The scale of manufacturing began to increase, led by Andrew Carnegie and his steel empire, and assisted by transport improvements which made it possible for the railroads to carry greater loads at higher speeds and for larger ships to carry increased cargoes.

Outside this national 'core', the Great Plains experienced a wave of settlement in the late nineteenth century, as dry-farming methods spread across the subhumid region. The mountains to the west were sprinkled with short-lived mining towns producing gold or silver at first, but then continuing with lead, zinc or copper as the railroads penetrated the region. On the west coast the timber in the north and some of the farming products in the south were beginning to attract new settlers, but the process was slow until the US Congress decided in 1902 to fund the extension of irrigation projects in a major way. Much of the land in this arid and mountainous west was not attractive to farmers and remained in the hands of the Federal government, or of the railroad companies which acquired it as a subsidy to cover their building costs. Large areas of unoccupied land remained between what were effectively oasis towns (Meinig, 1972). At the turn of the century the Federal government began to turn this land into National Forests and Parks, and to rent out the marginal grazing lands, where appropriate.

The South remained poor throughout this period, although cotton farming continued to be the main source of income, and its production was quadrupled after 1860 until the boll weevil struck in the early twentieth century. But cotton prices seldom produced a good income for the black tenant farmers, who descended into debts which tied them to their exhausted land. Some textile manufacturing grew up in the new southern towns such as Atlanta, but the majority of the population remained poor, and segregation of blacks was accomplished by a series of state laws which went uncontested by the Federal government. Blacks were effectively disenfranchised, and their economic and social opportunities restricted. The average income of people in the South fell to under a half of the US average, and remained there until the mid twentieth century.

The later nineteenth and early twentieth century thus saw the emergence of a new regional geography in the US, related closely to an almost total dominance of railroad transport, and to distinctive products of commercial farms and large factories. The relative concentration of wealth in the core region and the dependence of the peripheries was established. These regional distinctions were enhanced by increasing waves of immigrants from southern and eastern Europe to the northern cities, where cheap labour continued to be demanded by the expanding manufacturing industries. On the Pacific coast the building of the transcontinental railroads began a process of importing Chinese coolie labour, and chinatowns sprang up in San Francisco and elsewhere.

This period of late-nineteenth-century industrialisation affected farm, factory and personal mobility alike. Regional specialisation of agricultural products was possible with railroad transport of the crops to major markets, and so the 'Cotton Belt', 'Corn Belt' and 'Dairy Belt' could be distinguished. Mining and manufacturing regions further highlighted the economic differentiation of the nation which announced in 1890 that the frontier zone was no longer recognisable. A definite core zone around the north-eastern ports was expanding westwards through the manufacturing belt, but other parts were all peripheral in some way or other, and the South remained the most deprived region. This was the era when regions could be differentiated by a combination of economic and natural characteristics. Another feature of this time was the demise of medieval views of 'wilderness': once the frontier had closed, wilderness took on a new form in the minds of Americans – as a desirable change from the growing urbanisation of America. For the future, the infrastructure of the railroad age, and of the manufacturing towns in the north-east and north-centre, provided a built environment which inertia would maintain beyond its years of functional significance.

3.6 MID-TWENTIETH-CENTURY CHANGES

The period covering the late nineteenth century and early twentieth century ended with a series of distinctive, and largely economic, regions across the US. Their boundaries sometimes followed, and sometimes cut across, the major natural features. The first half of the twentieth century resulted in further changes of emphasis among the regions of the US, and in new economic and social processes which altered the basis of regional division (Figure 3.6).

Perhaps the most significant change was the growth of large metropolitan centres, in which the manufacturing and growing service industries were concentrated. These centres were closest together on the north-east coast, since the competition between the original port-cities had been maintained by the major four until they began to merge physically with each other. 'Megalopolis' was the name coined for this phenomenon by the French geographer, Jean Gottman, in 1957 (Gottman, 1961). The combination of so many multinational business headquarters, the financial institutions of New York and New England, the growing control of the

Comparative physical advantage increasing importance	Late-industrial capitalism Secondary sector =tertiary sector employment (primary small)	URBAN REGIONS
Growth of metropolitan centres plus suburban expansion		CENTRED ON METRO-
Very rapid increase in mobility Air, road, pipeline and improved rail, waterway	Republican system Increasing government intervention: State/county units less power, cities more	POLITAN CITIES

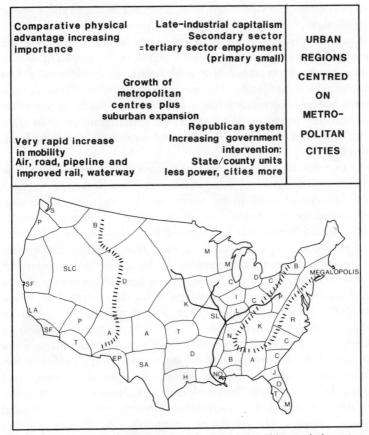

FIGURE 3.6   The regional geography of the US in the mid twentieth century. The letters are the initials of major metropolitan centres

expanding media, and the political centre of Washington DC, gave this urban conglomeration a unique place in the US and in the world. Large cities elsewhere in the US also expanded to engulf smaller surrounding towns. Rural areas by contrast withered in terms of employment opportunities and became the poorest parts of the nation.

The contrast between rural and metropolitan regions resulted from the availability of new modes of transport, such as the car, lorry, pipeline and aeroplane, which provided greater mobility and access to the variegated services of metropolitan centres. It also resulted from the switch out of occupations in the primary sector (with their rural locations) and into manufacturing, offices and shops (all essentially based in cities). It led to a new basis for regions: Megalopolis was indeed a region in its own right, but so were some of the other large cities with their commuting and commercial hinterlands. The metropolitan centres extended their influence into the surrounding areas, both as a source of homes for commuting workers and as a field for distributing products from local factories and the warehouses of national and international firms.

The twentieth century also witnessed the regeneration of the South and the growth of major new regions which began to rival the established 'core' in the north-east. By mid century the west coast became the major zone of attraction for internal migrants. The Second World War had resulted in the investment of facilities to provide war materials for use against Japan, and saw the growth of major industries which supported this. After the war economic growth continued and California grew to become the most populous and wealthy state in the US. By the 1970s the stream of migration to California was slowing due to some of the highest living costs in the nation (especially house prices). The Pacific north-west of Oregon and Washington changed its unattractive image for a desirable one by emphasising the importance of the quality of life. Isolation, a dull and rainy climate and a provincial image had dogged the north-west, but many of these features became attractive to the 1960s breed of recreation-oriented and ecology-minded young families. The change of perception was aided by a major surplus of clean and cheap hydro-electricity, and by the growth of the Boeing corporation and related manufacturing and commercial employers.

Those who moved to the west coast came from both the North and South of the eastern half of the US. Those from the North came from the older cities of the manufacturing belt, which had begun to experience a major series of structural economic changes. These changes included the increased costs of winter heating, and of energy in general, in the north-east. New England acquired a reputation as a run-down region with out-of-date manufacturing products, high living costs, and high levels of unemployment. The seeds of this began when the region failed to diversify from its early industrial base of textiles, leather and small-metal goods. It suffered greatly in the depression years of the 1930s and the impression was enhanced again in the 1950s after a period of wartime prosperity. Many farmers from the Midwest also moved farther west in their transition to urban living.

The South went through a major set of changes during this mid-twentieth-century period. The ties of debt which had prevented many poor rural blacks from moving out of the South were loosened by the predations of the boll weevil in the 1920s, the 1930 economic depression and the needs for labour in other parts of the nation during the Second World War: black families left the South for places perceived as providing greater opportunities. These places included the northern cities and the west coast. After 1920 the employers in the northern cities found their traditional sources of cheap labour – immigrants from Europe – cut off by new immigration laws. The blacks provided an answer to this problem, and the inner city ghettos began to expand and become overcrowded by turns. All major cities in the north-east and north-central sectors of the US had rapid increases of black population from 1920 to 1960, and by 1960 the largest numbers of American poor were concentrated in these inner city areas. The move to the west coast, and particularly to Los Angeles, by black people was somewhat later, and encouraged by the need for factory workers during the Second World War, but had a similar result on the major cities.

The South changed little until after the Second World War: the loss of large numbers of black families from the 1920s did not greatly alter the economic, social and political face of the region. During the war the South became the base for many military facilities and for others which clustered around the cheap Tennessee Valley Authority (TVA) power provision (e.g. Oak Ridge Atomic Research facility and Redstone Arsenal). After the war government programmes continued to favour the South, and there was also economic growth due to the exploitation of oil and gas along the Gulf coast, and to the expansion of textile manufacturing along the south-eastern piedmont zone. The civil rights agitation of the early 1960s reflected these changes and the declining role of traditional southern attitudes. The pleasant northern suburbs of booming Atlanta, the availability of air-conditioning, the relaxation of social and political curbs, and the economic growth of this region resulted in a process of population growth which included a major element of immigration from the North. The South started to change from a poverty-stricken and racially-segregated society to one which could begin to take advantage of the US affluence.

In addition to the changing economic patterns and their organisation across the US, new patterns based on distinctive populations emerged in the mid twentieth century. The 'melting-pot' thesis had applied quite well to the northern European groups reaching the US in large numbers up to the late nineteenth century: Dutch surnames are a feature of people living in Grand Rapids, Michigan; German surnames of Milwaukee, Wisconsin; and Scandinavian surnames of Minneapolis, Minnesota – but the people are 'normal' Americans. However, the black population had always remained a major exception to this concept. In 1900 nearly 90 per cent of the black population was still concentrated in the South, and the small numbers elsewhere were largely ignored. By the 1960s only half of the US black population remained in the South, and the other half lived very noticeably in northern and western inner-city areas. This movement visibly emphasised differences between Americans, and led to increased public concern over the lot of minority groups.

The Hispanic sector of the population also began to form an increasing and distinctive group. It had for long been strong in the south-west, since many Spanish-surname people had been living there when the US took over the territories in the 1840s, and Mexican peasants had provided a source of cheap migrant labour for farmers in the US states near the border. A major increase in the Hispanic population of these traditional areas and elsewhere in the US took place after the Second World War. Puerto Ricans flooded into New York and its environs and into Chicago in the 1950s, and Cuban refugees moved to Miami, Florida, following the Castro revolution in 1959. A wide variety of Latin Americans followed. The character of places such as southern Florida, southern Texas and southern California is made distinctive by the Spanish language signs and by a commercial provision which reflects this Hispanic presence.

Also particularly affecting the west coast are increasing numbers of Asians: the chinatowns have been joined by groups of Japanese, Philippinos and Vietnamese in particular. And, almost as a footnote, the aboriginal groups have been attempting to make more of their presence, especially in the US south-west and in Alaska. Land claims and water resource claims are before courts and

Congress, and these, if granted, would also change the character of the areas where amerinds and inuits are most numerous or have reservations. The decade of the 1970s witnessed the first increase in native American population since independence.

These mid-twentieth-century changes reflect the importance of changed economic and social conditions in the US and have resulted in yet another set of regional realities. The urban-industrial complex has come to dominate the geography of the nation. The increases in mobility provided by road and air transport have brought different patterns of commuting and different views of residential location possibilities. These trends have made the metropolitan hubs the focus of regional distinctiveness as much as environmental or economic product characteristics had an influence on earlier regional divisions. The region has become a functional, rather than a structural, concept.

As the trend to metropolitan scales of urban development, and the vastly increased levels of mobility, were taking place, the basic political units of county and state were beginning to look anachronistic (Meinig, 1972). 'Personal space', defined as bounded by common movements such as journeys to work, and those for shopping or leisure activities, increased greatly in scope and commonly encompassed several counties. The increasing mobility also meant that greater numbers of inter-state facilities required regulation or development at the Federal level, and this further enhanced the position and powers of the Federal government despite some attempts to return these powers to the state capitals.

3.7 THE EVOLVING MOSAIC OF REGIONS

By the mid twentieth century the pattern of regions in the US was that of a mosaic depending on a combination of natural, demographic, economic, social and political characteristics, together with distinctive variations related to the time and scale of settlement. Regions as recognised in the US today may be viewed as a series of overlays resulting from the changing processes of regional differentiation over time.

The aboriginal peoples were distributed, and adopted distinctive cultures, according to their close (almost symbiotic) relationship with the natural environment. The early European settlers brought very different cultural perceptions of the North American resources, but were at first limited by the difficulties of overland transport. By the mid eighteenth century the last arrivals, the British, had begun to dominate the political control of the continent, and further development became focused on the colonies of the Atlantic coast. During the early days of American independence there was a common push westwards from the east coast, and this increased in pace after the Civil War until the frontier lands were filled. By the late nineteenth century economic processes of regional differentiation became dominant. The early part of the twentieth century witnessed the growth of major metropolitan centres and the concentration of economic, social and political life in these centres.

Such changing sets of processes provide only a crude means for distinguishing between the varied time periods which have had a changing influence on the evolution of regions in the US. They can, however, be applied to each of the most commonly recognised regions of the nation. Thus, New England is made distinctive by its combination of glacially-eroded hills and uneven valley-floor gradients; by its occupation by eastern woodland amerinds and later by the puritan settlers from England; by its early involvement with manufacturing and its subsequent inertia in the twentieth century until the major structural change into high-technology manufacturing and the growth of higher education facilities led to an economic revival. All these phases have left their marks on the landscape and people, and on the economic, social and political environment of New England. The Middle Atlantic was settled later, in different ways, and its cities grew to dominate the colonies and early republic; like New England it was involved in the early manufacturing phase, but tended to keep up with new developments more effectively due to competition between the main centres of population for the lucrative trade links with the interior. Despite castigation as the 'Frostbelt' in the 1970s, this region remained the 'control centre' of the nation with a political, financial and cultural lead. At the other end of the US the west coast has fewer of the artefacts resulting from an early occupation: only a tiny relic of Spanish occupation vies with the mid-twentieth-century built environment and the irrigated farmlands in producing the distinctiveness of this region.

This approach can be extended to all parts of the US at various scales. Each region has a set of overlays of landscape elements which have accumulated from a set of different regional geographies over time. At each period of history there has been a different interaction between natural, economic, social and political factors.

3.8 CONCLUSIONS

The distinctive sets of regions which have evolved at each stage of US history may thus be superimposed on each other. This process emphasises the present distinctiveness of each part of the nation, since there is a progressive manner in which the relics of each stage affect the present regional geography. Cities in the north-east are quite different from those in the south-west, since they retain extensive tracts of nineteenth-century worker tenements and factories surrounding the city centre, together with older remnants of their mercantile-age port and trading functions: the historic district of Philadelphia and downtown Boston provide examples. In the south-west cities some remnants of Spanish/Mexican regimes are often preserved, but there was minimal late-nineteenth-century industrialisation, and there is a rapid transition from the historic cores and central business districts into 1920s and more recent suburbs. Related differences can also be detected in rural areas from their field patterns and buildings (Stilgoe, 1982).

The overlays of landscape features – roads, railroads, field systems, residential lots, central business districts – also reflect the changing and developing social structures and social value systems. The varied American landscapes and regions over time reflect the changes from environment-related subsistence to agricultural and urban-industrial capitalism. These changes have involved new technologies and shifts in employment structure. So much is clear from this chapter, but there remains a danger that the individual human decisions tend to become lost in such a general account. It is important to record that, throughout the period referred to, individual people have had major impacts on the geographical expression of regional differences and on the innovations in ideas and values which caused each stage in cultural development to give way to the next.

4. One America?

4.1 INTRODUCTION

Having recognised the importance of regional differences due to natural resource occurrence, the distribution of people, and varied patterns of historical evolution, the question arises as to whether these differences are decreasing at the present time. It may be the case that the reduced interest in regional studies among geographers reflects reality and that regional differences are becoming of less significance to society. However, if the regional concept is to be of renewed importance to geographical studies, and if the arguments of regionalism are to carry weight, both must have a basis in continuing local and regional socio-economic distinctiveness.

4.2 EVIDENCE FOR THE ONENESS OF LIFE IN THE US

The US society of the late twentieth century is one in which many features of human interaction are becoming similar across the nation and are reflected in common artefacts – buildings, advertising hoardings, recreation facilities. Long-distance travel, particularly by air, is a common part of life in the US, and most parts of the nation are within a few hours' travel of each other. Families think little of a car journey from the Midwest to Florida for a 'spring break' of a few days. Wherever such travellers choose to go, much will be familiar to them, due to the mass marketing and mass communications which have been a feature of national life. Even as late as 1970 a small number of local TV channels and local supermarket groups were still in existence, but now by the mid 1980s the TV fare is similar across the nation and so are the supermarkets – as well as the fast-food chains and other commercial outlets.

To accompany this attention of the commercial world to cultivating similar tastes in the whole population across America, there has been a convergence of values, economies and experiences for individuals. The regional average per capita income differences widened until 1920, and since then have converged (Figure 4.1): at their greatest separation the range was between less than 50 per cent of the US average (South) to over 50 per cent above. Today the differences between the nine divisions recognised by the Bureau of Census are restricted to 10 per cent above and 20 per cent below the norm. At the beginning of the twentieth century there was a major distinction between manufacturing and non-manufacturing regions, and between regions with distinctive types of manufacturing. Today many of these differences have vanished, or have been reduced, since electrical power is available almost everywhere, and the older place-specific factories have given way to types of manufacturing which could be sited almost anywhere in the nation with little difference in total costs.

The smaller degree to which people are tied to a location has been enhanced by greater personal mobility and also by the introduction of retirement pensions on a major scale: although introduced in the 1930s, they came to wide fruition in the 1960s and after. For these reasons a greater proportion of the population can now live away from the metropolitan focus of employment opportunities, and increasing affluence allows many more to afford second homes in scenic, rural mountain areas. These trends all lead to a broader spread of wealth and spending power across regions.

The core-periphery economic distinctions of the earlier part of the twentieth century have also given way to a new set of regional relationships. At that stage the north-eastern seaboard from Washington DC to Boston, and the manufacturing belt extending through Pittsburgh and Detroit to Chicago, could have been regarded as the national core. Now there would be debate at least that there are other cores in southern California, Dallas/Houston and possibly Atlanta and Miami. In addition, the original core of national economic and political activity is now a region which is losing population, although its proportion of the national income and political power is reacting to other forces which have tended to centralise it still in the Washington–New York–Boston corridor.

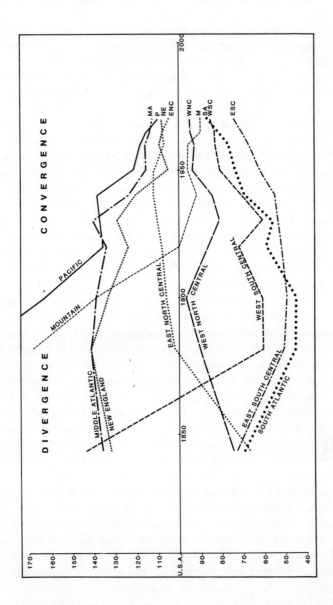

There are thus signs that some of the economic differences which marked off regions in the past are now less significant within the United States. The growing role of the Federal government, the single national market and the complexity of internal movements of people and goods have all increased the possibility of action, and the significance of issue studies at a national scale. The United States has also had to act as the major power in the non-Communist world, and this has further enhanced the powers of the Federal government at the expense of the states and local government.

4.3 EVIDENCE FOR THE PERSISTENCE OF REGIONAL DIFFERENCES

Despite all the evidence which would suggest that the US is moving towards a homogeneous society in which regions as such do not exist, and that the main geographical distinctiveness is now between town and country, there are many other differences which persist and have a regional or local expression in the lives of the people or in the landscapes. The evidence for the convergence of economic conditions across the nation is paralleled by other evidence which demonstrates a continuing differentiation in relation to environmental, social and political criteria.

It is still possible to categorise regions on the basis of characteristics of natural features and environments, or demographic composition of the population, or to some extent on economic conditions. Thus, the extremes of Florida, Alaska, New England, the flat Midwest, and the arid/mountainous south-west, are clearly set apart from each other and can be described in terms which makes each unique in its own environmental 'back-drop'. This is not only a consideration of static characteristics of the natural environment in a scenic sense, but also involves the changing types of interaction between human activities and each environment. Such interactions are often specific to the local conditions, such as

FIGURE 4.1 The divergence of personal income by region in the nineteenth century, and convergence in the twentieth century. The figures are proportions of the US average (= 100) per capita income

the draining of the Everglades to produce muck-soil farmland, or the construction of the oil pipeline across the permafrost of Alaska. Whereas the value of the natural environment was formerly perceived in terms of the quality of the soil, and the type and amount of mineral resources, as a basis for the production of food and manufactured goods, a new element has been added in terms of its value as recreational amenity. This has altered the perception of many regions from unattractive to attractive for residence. Differences in the natural environments thus continue to introduce an important element of regional distinctiveness.

The most important socio-economic differences between regions are those which are based on inequalities which emerge between groups of people and so between the regions in which they live. Affluent America still contains many examples of those who have been left behind in the general advance to greater affluence. There are the amerinds on their reservations, the remaining blacks in the rural South and their counterparts in the inner cities, and also some of the Hispanic and other racial or ethnic minorities – often crowded into the poorer parts of the major cities. Although generally true, it is not always the non-white minorities who come off worst. There are also those who may have white skins, but who have not yet made the move from rural to urban functional systems, and remain behind in the places where there are few jobs, or only poorly paying ones: these conditions are common where subsistence farming has been displaced in upland regions, as in much of Appalachia, the Ozarks or the Upper Great Lakes, or in marginal farming regions in the Great Plains. Another group with low incomes is the elderly, although for many of these a retirement pension may be generous, and their incomes have to be seen in the light of the fact that many will have completed paying for the upbringing of their children and for their house. This means that large numbers of the elderly may have a greater proportion of disposable income than the younger family heads. The distribution of these disadvantaged groups is less by large-scale regions than formerly, and so the spatial incidence of poverty does not coincide with the major regional divisions: it may be masked by them.

The concentration of the wealthier families contrasts with those with little material wealth. Most of the former are to be found in the larger cities, and particularly in very distinctive inner-city areas or in the outer suburbs. Thus, inner Boston is the home for some very poor black people, with restricted access to education, health facilities and jobs. It also has very wealthy districts, such as the Back Bay and Beacon Hill areas, close to the centre. Only a few miles away in the suburbs there are some of the richest communities in America, with the highest density of doctors to serve them and some of the best-funded high schools in the nation. The social and political differences between these districts within a single metropolitan area emphasise the significance of spatial differences and the interlocking scales of activity at local, regional and national levels.

4.4 REGIONS IN THE POST-INDUSTRIAL SOCIETY

The United States has been identified as the first nation in the world to enter the 'post-industrial society', and the present changes in its regional geography can be examined in this context. The onset of the post-industrial society involves a massive shift in economic and social structure which will have an increasing impact on the nation's geography: distributions of people, economic activity and residential locations are changing and, if the thesis followed in the previous chapter is true, it would be expected that this would produce new patterns of regional advantage and disadvantage (Figure 4.2).

The economic changes include the growth of employment in the tertiary sector compared with the primary or secondary sectors, so that the tertiary sector accounts for 75 per cent or more of total employment in the mid 1980s. There are many more jobs in the professions. There is also an emphasis on high-technology industry with an investment in research and development to generate new innovative products. The social changes are related to increased levels of education, leisure and affluence: the work-orientated and achievement-orientated values and residential locations are replaced by a greater concern for amenity and access to recreational opportunities. Such a new society and its geography do not happen at once, neither do they totally remove the artefacts of previous societies, and so the late twentieth century may be viewed as transitional between the high mass-consumption society with its metropolitan base and the new post-industrial society.

The apparent paradox involving the convergence of economic

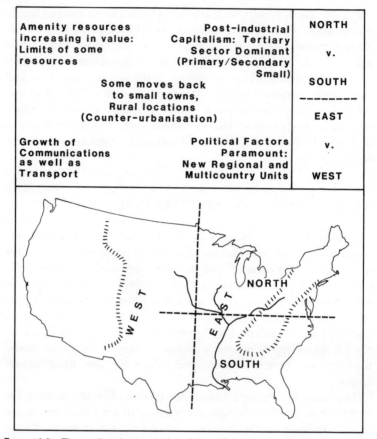

FIGURE 4.2   The regional geography of the US in the late twentieth century

life-styles and the continuing distinctiveness of regions within the US, described at the start of this chapter, may be partly explained by reference to this transitional stage reached at present in the move towards a post-industrial society. This can be demonstrated by a number of the trends evident since the mid 1970s. The 1970s witnessed some major changes in the distribution of Americans: the rate of population growth declined rapidly due to low birth rates, and immigration became the main factor in overall growth; the movement of people to cities was slowed and more moved out to suburbs and rural areas in the process of counter-urbanisation; and the core of older industrial growth in the north-east began to stagnate, while the South and West became the main population growth regions. This process has been described as 'the United States turning itself upside down and inside out' (Clark, 1985).

Another trend has involved changes in employment patterns and locations: new industries have new requirements in raw materials, capital and labour; the wider availability of energy, together with better transport systems, has presented a new set of locational possibilities; and the traditional centres of employment are perceived as having an obsolescent environment and high energy and labour costs. This is not just a matter of evening out the differences between former core and periphery, but is producing a fresh set of locational factors. Manufacturing, for instance, is no longer the main source of employment growth, and its relative contribution is declining. These changes challenge the basis of previous attempts at economic analysis of regional change (Clark *et al.*, 1986). The new factors tend to favour the South and West, and their more recent infrastructure, at the expense of the north-east.

Such changes have led to the new patterns of growing and declining regions across the nation. For those who can afford it, the US provides a similar range of services and facilities throughout the nation, mobility is easy and relatively cheap, and the life-styles of the moderately and very wealthy are not too different. For those who are discriminated against by the system, there is a more restricted existence in terms of places to live, or of jobs which are available or accessible. Social distance and space is so much smaller for the latter groups than the former. And yet the groups often exist in close contact: the subway which takes the middle-class commuters out of central New York has to pass through Harlem and the Bronx.

Another feature of this post-industrial society is the increasing complexity of relationships within a vast nation where relative distances have been reduced by modern transport and communications. This complexity suggests that the free market system may have problems in making the adjustments to an increasingly rapid pace of change, and that government co-ordination will be required to a greater extent. This century has seen an increase of Federal government involvement in many aspects of American life. Although the Reagan administration has rejected this notion, and particularly the concept of national planning through a set of regional commissions, which had been proposed at the end of the 1970s, it is likely that its approach is merely a temporary reaction against the growing role of central government.

4.5 CONCLUSIONS

It is clear, then, that although there have been a number of changes in the US since the Second World War which have favoured a nationwide unity of culture and economy, there are still many local and regional distinctions. In fact, many of the changes within the US are best studied at the regional level. Thus, while there are changes of population trends at the national level, it is particularly important to understand how the changes in population affect the regions. Similarly, energy- and water-resource policies are also national issues, but have important local and regional dimensions which cannot be ignored.

The fullest understanding of the society and culture of the United States can only be understood when unity at the national scale is combined with a study of regional diversity. The important point is that each issue has its most appropriate level for study and for action. This emphasises the fact that the tools of regional analysis are flexible – and also quite different from the traditional regional geography, which became almost a game of recognising unique units which reflected different usage by people of the earth's surface. Once recognised, these units became fixed, whereas there is a need to view them from the standpoint of changing process and relationships with other regions.

As the post-industrial society gains momentum it may be more appropriate to adopt a new pattern of regions in the study of the United States in order to demonstrate how the new sets of social and economic processes are affecting the nation. This could involve a combination of major regions and more local divisions. The major regions could be those adopted by the Bureau of Census, since their political and data-gathering base reflects the importance of public policy and information in the new society. The local divisions could be groups of counties outside the metropolitan centres, or specific sectors within the metropolitan centres which reflected the contrasting well-being of the people.

This discussion of the nature of the factors giving rise to regional changes in the United States at the end of the twentieth century has introduced a further factor which is important in an understanding of the contribution of regional studies. Regional differences are viewed not merely as a matter of varied distributions of natural resources, nor as one of differently perceived landscapes and living environment evolving over time, but as changing responses to dominant socio-economic systems. The pre-European, colonial, early industrial, high mass-consumption industrial and post-industrial societies all generated distinctive geographies with their own regional distinctions and relative importances of these regions within the nation (or continent before the nation was established). Such a concept enhances the value of regional studies and lifts them to a functional and explanatory level, which provides a basis for regionalism.

PART II: THE CONCERNS OF REGIONALISM

5. 'Frostbelt v. Sunbelt': a Particular Case

5.1 INTRODUCTION: A TALE OF TWO REGIONS?

The term 'Sunbelt' has had wide popular usage since the mid 1970s. It has been traced back to the conservative political analyst, K. Philips, who identified what he saw as a major change in balance between the Democratic and Republican parties at the end of the 1960s in his book, *The Emerging Republican Majority* (1969). Former Democratic party strongholds in the South and West were becoming Republican in their sympathies for the first time for many years. His 'Sunbelt' extended from the Carolinas to California, but excluded the Appalachian and Ozark Mountains (Figure 5.1).

The popularisation of the 'Sunbelt' concept in the 1970s resulted in a less clear definition of the region concerned and of the basis of using the idea. Some writers have extended the area covered up to Washington DC in the east and to Oregon and even Washington in the north-west. Others have defined the realm more narrowly – some down to the essentially Gulf Coast region from Florida to Texas, the 'South-east Metropolitan Sunshine Crescent'.

At the same time, the 'Sunbelt' has been seen as a concept which requires an oppositional idea, and terms such as 'Frostbelt', 'Snowbelt' and 'Rustbelt' have been coined to emphasise the contrast between the apparently positive and growing southern parts of the United States and the older Manufacturing Belt area of the north-eastern and north-central regions. This contrast was blown up into 'The Second War Between the States' in a *Business Week* article in May 1976. Economic and political sensitivities were jolted into facing up to the changes identified in this debate, and so issues of regionalism were highlighted.

The differences in definition reflect the variety of aspects of

69

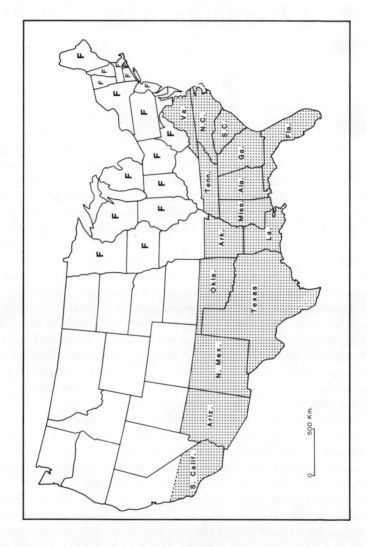

American life which have attempted to develop the concept in relation to their own particular interests. In addition to the political dimensions, there are implications for population movements and other aspects of demography; for economic changes in terms of regions of 'growth' and 'decline'; for social movements; for differences in religious expression; for the development of the urban built-environment and life-styles; and for popular perceptions, or images, of places. And there is also a strong element of 'physical determinism' implied in the use of the term.

An assessment of the significance of the 'Sunbelt' concept is thus of importance both to an understanding of the United States in the 1980s, and also to a fuller appreciation of the distinction between regional analysis and regionalism. This particular study also makes it possible to establish links between analytical regional studies and active regionalism. It is approached by way of some of the measures of change, which are then placed in historical context and evaluated in terms of their significance.

5.2 THE SYMPTOMS OF REGIONAL CHANGE

5.2.1 Political changes

The political changes identified by Philips have become real, but are linked to other major symptoms of change affecting the regional balance within the United States. The political changes involved two major shifts – of the numbers elected to the House of Representatives in Washington, and of their political allegiance.

The numbers of congressional representatives in the House is based on the Census of Population taken every ten years, and reapportionment takes place on the basis of this. The number of representatives has remained at 435 since 1910. Any shift of regional emphasis in the House thus reflects significant relative population changes. In 1940 the North-east and Midwest regions of the US were still dominant, with 251 seats to 185 in the rest of the nation. By 1980 the position had changed, with 208 seats remaining

FIGURE 5.1 The 'Sunbelt' as defined by Phillips, and the states included in the 'Frostbelt' (F). The states surrounding the Gulf of Mexico have also been termed the 'Southeast Metro Sunshine Crescent'

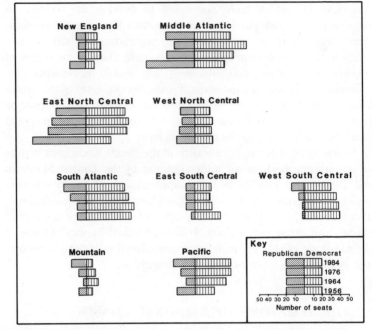

FIGURE 5.2 Changing regional allegiance in the US House of Representatives, 1956–84. D = Democrat, R = Republican. See Figure 1.1 for map of divisions

in the North-east and Midwest, while the rest of the US had 226. The main changes over this period were gains of 22 seats in California, 13 seats in Florida and 6 seats in Texas, while losses were concentrated in New York (11 seats) and Pennsylvania (10 seats). Few of the other 'Sunbelt' states gained representatives individually, and some lost them. The population changes will be examined in more detail, but it is clear that on the measure of representation on the federal legislative body, three states (California, Florida and Texas) play major parts (94 seats between them, 22 per cent of the total), which were formerly the province of

FIGURE 5.3 The membership of State legislatures, 1984. Each State has two houses, reflecting the Federal Senate and House of Representatives. This map shows how the Democrats retain control of the South at this level

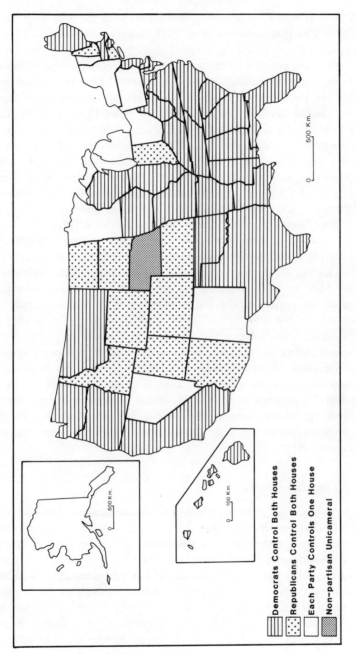

Democrats Control Both Houses

Republicans Control Both Houses

Each Party Controls One House

Non-partisan Unicameral

New York and Pennsylvania (78 seats between them in 1940, 57 in 1980). The reapportionment of 1982, based on the 1980 Census of Population, continued this trend.

When the changes in the political geography of the United States are examined in terms of party allegiance, it has to be remembered that the Democratic Party was essentially an alliance of northern liberals and southern conservatives from the 1930s to 1980. The Republican Party has been dominated by moderately conservative influences over this period. In 1940 the South was still virtually a one-party region, and the real elections took place for the Democratic nomination. At this time 87 per cent of the southern seats in the US House of Representatives were Democrats. Northern Democrats were less conspicuous and formed scarcely 40 per cent of those elected from the North-east and Midwest (Figure 5.2). By 1980 there had been major changes in this pattern: Democrats elected from the South made up only 65 per cent of the total from that region, while they became the majority party in the North-east and Midwest with just over 55 per cent of the seats. Over this period the pattern in the West fluctuated, but Democrats held 53 per cent of the seats in both 1940 and 1980. So the main shift of allegiance was between the northern and southern parts of the eastern half of the nation. The breakdown of the one-party system in the South, and the greater prominence of northern Democrats suggests major social and economic changes as well as these political symptoms of change. A similar pattern of change can be discerned in the membership of the US Senate, although the representation in the state legislatures still reflects older realities (Figure 5.3).

5.2.2 Population changes

The population changes which are behind some of these facts of political representation also demonstrate that rapid growth and decline were restricted to a few states. Thus, between 1970 and 1980, California, Florida and Texas together recorded 42 per cent of the total population growth in the United States: they each had population increases of approximately 3 million. A further ten states (AZ, CO, GA, LA, NC, OR, SC, TN, VA, WA) had individual increases of 0.5–1 million people, and a total of 30 per cent of the overall US increase. Of these thirteen states which had nearly three-quarters of the US population increase in the 1970s, only Oregon and Washington are outside the 'Sunbelt'.

In the period since 1980 these trends have continued and intensified. Between 1980 and 1983, California, Florida and Texas grew by a total of nearly 4 million people (53 per cent of total US growth), while the next ten states (Oklahoma replacing Tennessee) added nearly 3 million (39 per cent of total US growth). Thus 92 per cent of net population growth in the early 1980s occurred in just thirteen states.

Much of this population change involved migration (Figure 5.4): in the 1970s over 5.5 million people left the North-east and Midwest, mainly from New York, Ohio, Illinois, Pennsylvania and Michigan (77 per cent of the total migration losses from 22 states). The South gained nearly 6 million migrants (Florida 2.5 million and Texas 1.5 million) and the West just over 4 million (California 1.75 million). In the early 1980s the North-east and Midwest lost a further 1.5 million outmigrants while the South gained 2.25 million and the West 1.25 million. This was an increased rate of migration out of the Midwest and into the South (from losses of 270,000 per year in the 1970s to over 400,000 per year from 1980–3 in the Midwest, and from gains of 600,000 per year to over 700,000 in the South), but the rate of outmigration from the North-east slowed down, and the rate of inmigration to the West remained stable.

It is important to put the scale of these changes into perspective. The migrations from the North-east and Midwest in the 1970s involved under 5 per cent of the populations of those regions, and did not totally cancel out the natural increase in the 1970s or early 1980s. Inmigration added less than 10 per cent to the population of the South over the decade of the 1970s – only just over half the total population increase. During the 1970s the two northern regions lost some 5 million by migration in a 1980 population of 109 million; the South gained nearly 6 million and the West 4 million.

The difference between the losses and gains is accounted for by immigration from abroad into the United States. Immigrants had been concentrated in the northern parts of the nation until 1920, and then had fallen to low totals through times of restricted immigration, economic depression and the Second World War. But after 1950 the majority of migrants came in via the southern and western margins of the nation. Mexicans entered the south-west in

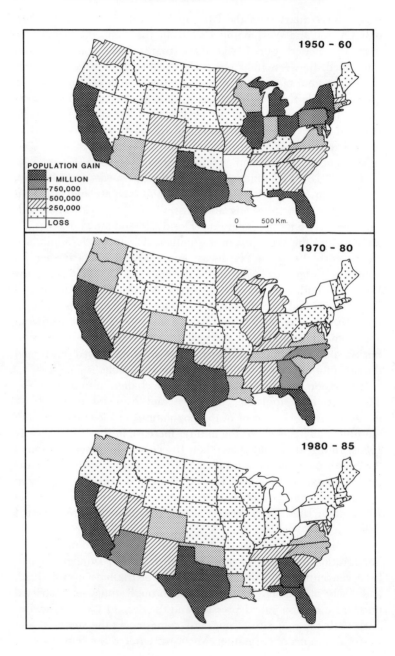

increasing numbers, but Cubans also came into Florida and Puerto Ricans into northern cities, so that the Hispanic element in the population grew to provide a distinctive characteristic of many southern parts of the US (Figure 5.5). Furthermore, increasing numbers of people of Asiatic origin entered the western parts. Although these groups began to move throughout the US, most remained concentrated in the South and West and accounted for a large part of the additions by migrant groups.

Another important trend within the US population structure was that black people stopped migrating from the South to northern cities in the 1970s – at least, the net migration showed a small move back to the South, and the total amount of such migration was small compared to the 1950s and 1960s.

Just as the political changes reflected population changes, so the population changes reflect other economic and social trends within the US. It is important to delve beneath the facts and figures and attempt to assess the factors behind the changes taking place.

5.2.3. Economic shifts

The Sunbelt–Frostbelt tension can also be used as a basis for identifying changing trends in the US economy. As late as 1970 the southern states could be shown to lag behind the rest of the US in terms of individual income and socio-economic well-being. In the South as a whole in 1970 per capita personal incomes were 86 per cent of the US average, but this ranged from 75 per cent in the East South Central (only 65 per cent in the poorest state of Mississippi) to 91 per cent in the South Atlantic. By 1980 the South had per capita incomes which were 92 per cent of the US

FIGURE 5.4 Population changes in the US, 1950–85, summarised in three periods:
(A) 1950–60: maximum growth took place in the 'Manufacturing Belt' states of the North-east, and slow growth in the South outside of Florida, Texas and California
(B) 1970–80: little growth in the 'Manufacturing Belt'; maximum growth in the South. (1960–70 was transitional between (A) and (B))
(C) 1980–5: (values half the key in relation to 5-year period) shows heavy losses in the 'Manufacturing Belt' and increasing growth in the south-west

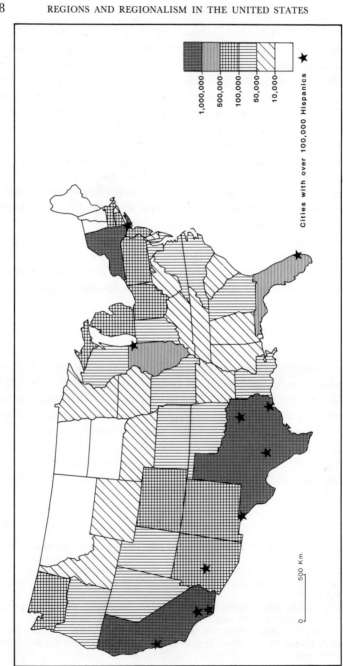

average, with 78 per cent in the East South Central Division (69 per cent in Mississippi) and 94 per cent in the South Atlantic. Over the same period the above-average per capita incomes of the North-east fell closer to the US norm, further reducing the disparity between these regions. A wider range of indicators of socio-economic well-being has been combined in a single index in Figure 5.6. This also demonstrates a major shift between Frostbelt and Sunbelt during the 1970s.

This disparity had been a feature of the North–South contrast since the Civil War. For over a hundred years the southern states had been the poorest part of the US, left as a decaying rural wilderness as its chief source of income – the cotton crop – was devastated by the boll weevil and poor farm management in the early twentieth century. Manufacturing produced wealth in the North, and the South was treated as a colonial empire by the North until after the Second World War. However, since mid century manufacturing employment has become dominant in most southern states: two of them, North and South Carolina, now have a higher proportion of their working population in manufacturing than any other US state. The south-eastern part of the US has become a new 'manufacturing belt'.

For long the South had a poor industrial mix, lacking the basic manufacturing industries which had been established in the North, and dependent on the low-wage manufacturing of textiles, tobacco and furniture-making. Since 1950 these industries have been developed further, together with chemical industries (based on local oil, gas, sulphur, phosphates and wood), government contracts (especially in relation to the NASA space programme) and related electronics industries. These industries have smaller and more widely dispersed factories than those which developed in the North from the later part of the nineteenth century, and so produce different landscapes and rely less on local concentrations of labour.

By contrast the old manufacturing belt in the North, despite continuing decline in manufacturing employment, still had 8.7 million jobs in manufacturing (42 per cent US total, producing 47 per cent of the value added by industry). The long-established

FIGURE 5.5 The distribution of Hispanic people in the US: they are more highly concentrated in major cities than other groups

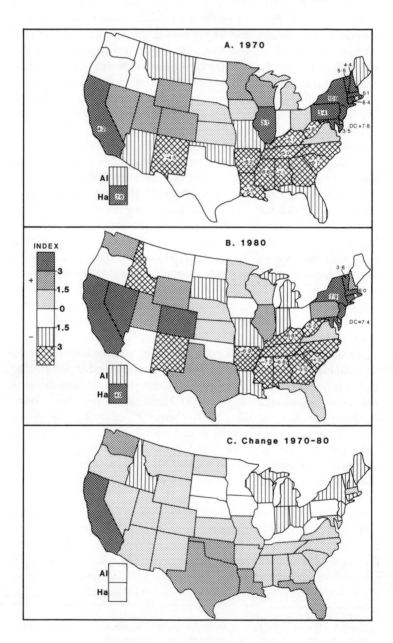

metal-working and mechanical engineering industries are still important there, with a major emphasis on transport equipment in the Midwest. This region has also taken a major part in the development of the electronics industries. The metal-working and mechanical engineering industries tend to require large factories and sites close to the labour and product markets of the largest metropolitan centres. Particular centres within the northern manufacturing belt tend to specialise, and are hit by recessions: the traumas of, firstly, the steel region around Pittsburgh and, in the 1970s, the car-manufacturing region around Detroit, illustrate this point.

The northern and southern manufacturing belts are thus different in character. Apart from the textile industries, there has been little direct movement of manufacturing industries from the Frostbelt to the Sunbelt. Some of the industries concentrated in the North have been declining due to the changing structure of manufacturing industry as a whole. The newer industries, and particularly those looking for cheap labour to staff their production units (as opposed to research units and corporate headquarters), have been established in the South – in preference to going overseas to Taiwan or Singapore. However, other changes taking place in the South have reduced this advantage of lower wages than the North, and the recession of the early 1980s has demonstrated that the type of manufacturing established in the Sunbelt is often vulnerable to market changes. By 1986 unemployment levels had been reversed compared to the early 1970s, and the southern states had increasing levels while the lowest levels were to be found in the north-east (particularly New England). Perhaps this foreshadows a further reversal of the fortunes of the North and South, and shows that the 'Sunbelt' phenomenon is a temporary one.

Another feature of shifts in employment may be even more significant. Virtually all the 'new' jobs created in the United States

---

FIGURE 5.6 Socio-economic well-being in the US, 1970–80. The index is compiled from nine variables (family income, unemployment, education, health care, public assistance, housing environment, access to recreation opportunities, crime rate, bank deposits). Plus values are above average and minus below average. The maps for 1970 and 1980 demonstrate the changes in well-being for each state, and the map of change shows the extent of shifts in well-being during the decade

since 1960 have been in the service sector (i.e. retail and wholesale trade; finance, insurance and real estate; business and personal services; and professions). While the US population rose from 179 million in 1960 to 236 million in 1984, employment in manufacturing rose from 17 to 19 million but employment in services rose from 34 to 70 million. Although the southern states are relatively poor in terms of service jobs compared to other parts of the US, they do not lag far behind. It is this change which has been so revolutionary within the South, and has led to many moving into the Sunbelt to take up managerial and professional jobs since the 1960s.

It is particularly significant that economic growth in the Sunbelt is concentrated in and around major cities such as those in Florida, Atlanta, Houston, Dallas—Fort Worth and Los Angeles. This is where the service industries are most sophisticated and best developed.

A further aspect of this development of new types of employment has been in the mushrooming growth of government employment, both at the Federal and at the state and local levels. The Federal presence in the South began to rise before the Second World War with such projects as the Tennessee Valley Authority and increasing numbers of military bases, which have remained important. Since the 1950s there has been a massive expansion of state and local government employment, which has affected every part of the United States.

5.2.4 Social and political changes

It is difficult to tell whether the major social changes in much of the Sunbelt – but especially in the Old South – are due to these economic shifts, or to the imposition of civil rights legislation. Certainly, many of the former restrictive practices applied to black people have been removed and after a period of informal continued application easier relationships now exist between racial groups in the South. Many blacks who moved to northern cities after 1920, and especially after 1950, have returned to the South and find it preferable to live there than in the northern city ghettos where job opportunities have been drastically reduced in the 1980s.

The influx of people to the Sunbelt has changed the patterns of politics: the professional incomers have often been able to disturb the cosy one-party establishment which existed, and have opened up opportunities for a wider group than the cronies of those in power. This has released much of the South from a formerly feudal system, and has made it more attractive for new people to settle.

Another major feature which has been effective in the Sunbelt is its increasing choice as a place to retire. It was only from the 1960s that large numbers of retirees were able to move to warmer climes after a lifetime of labour in the manufacturing cities of the North. But many have taken that opportunity since, and much of Florida is devoted to catering for their needs. Other centres have been established around the Gulf of Mexico and through Arizona into southern California. This phenomenon has also had a major effect on the demography and economy of the Sunbelt states.

5.2.5 A new level of urban life

The increasing population and developing economy of the Sunbelt has been paralleled by mainly urban growth. The new cities of the Sunbelt have struck observers as different from those in the North-east and Midwest (Brunn and Wheeler, 1980). In fact, they exhibit many of the features of metropolitan centres elsewhere in the US, but have smaller developments of inner-city worker housing related to the main phase of manufacturing development in the late nineteenth century. Another feature of the newer cities is that they are often less hampered by the maze of jurisdictions which are a feature of northern cities and which hamper overall metropolitan planning as the inhabitants of wealthy suburbs resist plans for financial support of inner-city services. Sunbelt cities such as Atlanta have become attractive places to live in – particularly in the wealthy white suburban sections. A 1985 study by the National Planning Association forecast that half of the new jobs created up to the year 2000 would be in 30 metropolitan areas in the US, with all but 7 in the Sunbelt (Figure 5.7). As with other data on the Sunbelt, there is a conspicuous concentration of these growth cities in California, Texas and Florida.

However, all cities and their built environments reflect the times in which they experienced a major expansion: growth in the Sunbelt took place at a time when inter-state highways facilitated auto-mobility and out-of-town commercial services, and when many of the poor were streaming northwards to join their apparently better-off relations. Local businessmen took up boosterish attitudes

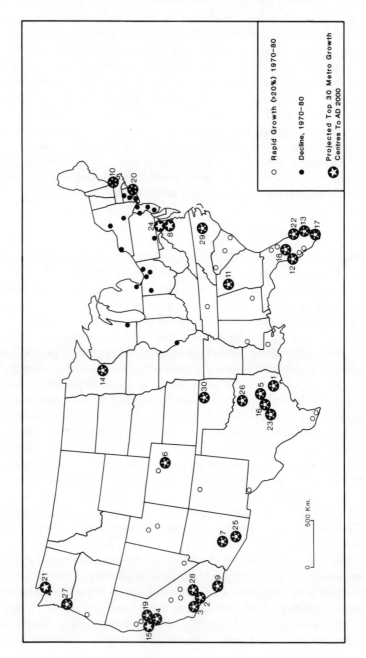

and sank large sums into redeveloping the central areas of their cities, together with the building of lavish airport facilities. More recently there have been signs that Sunbelt cities will be overtaken by difficulties which have affected northern cities – as outer suburbs refuse to be incorporated within the larger city, and as some of the older inner suburbs begin to show signs of decay.

5.3 WHAT LIES BEHIND THE SUNBELT CONCEPT?

The consideration of this phenomenon so far has shown that the inter-regional contrasts which have led to the designation of 'Sunbelt' and 'Frostbelt' are based on broad generalisations, which are often difficult to pursue at the local level. But even at the most general level it is clear that changes have taken place. Various explanations have been offered for the contrasts noted.

5.3.1 The climatic conditions

The very terms indicate a link with climate, but such a deterministic line of reasoning is difficult to press home as the sole factor affecting the noted changes. Certainly, the Sunbelt zone is the warmest part of the US. This has allowed an opposition to be established between a perceived 'frontier of comfort' of the southern margins of the US and a 'frontier of hardship' farther north. The winters of the Sunbelt zone are relatively mild, and the development of domestic air-conditioning has made it possible to endure the hot humidity of the Gulf coasts and the extremely high temperatures of the Arizona desert. However, the low winter heating bills may be offset by high costs of summer air-conditioning. There has been a long-established tradition of sanatoria and retirement residence for the richer people in both Florida and the south-west, and this prospect has recently been extended to larger numbers of the US population due to the wide availability of pensions.

But climate is only a part of the more general amenity factor – access to mountains and lakes, sea and forest – allied to lower costs

FIGURE 5.7 Population changes in US metropolitan areas since 1970 (after D. Clark, and *US News & World Report,* 18 March 1985)

of land and building and easier telecommunications with home and family in other parts of the nation. These 'pull' factors contrast with the 'push' of unattractive old industrial cities with abandoned and rusting plant in the north and unreclaimed waste heaps surrounding them, as well as with the longer winters in the Frostbelt.

5.3.2 Catching up, or becoming more different?

Many evaluations of the Sunbelt phenomenon tend to be purely economic in outlook. Even within this discipline there have been disagreements on what the movements charted signify. One group of economists believes that they reflect a convergence of conditions across the nation, but others feel that regions are growing apart. There is evidence to support both arguments.

The model of economic convergence is based on the belief that the economy can be controlled best at the national level, and that growth rates will tend to converge over time between regions within a nation. Thus the nineteenth-century and early-twentieth-century growth in the North-east and Midwest regions of the US has been offset by more recent growth in the Far West and South. Eventually growth in these regions will slow down, and others (including the older regions) will advance more rapidly with increasingly equal conditions across the US. It can be shown that average regional per capita incomes have indeed converged in this century following nineteenth-century differentiation (Figure 4.1). There are also indications that growth in California is beginning to slow down, while the decline evident in New England in the mid twentieth century is beginning to be arrested and reversed.

And yet, this may be too much of a generalisation. Most of the variation in regional income differences earlier in the twentieth century was accounted for by the deprived and stunted South which remained largely rural for much longer than the rest of the US. Growth since 1930 in the South has been due to a combination of low-wage manufacturing and government investment in such projects as TVA, the National Aeronautics and Space Administration (NASA) developments and many military bases. There has also been a growth of other 'transfer' income in the form of retirement pension cheques posted from northern cities to the Sunbelt-based retirees. The convergence might therefore be based on rather

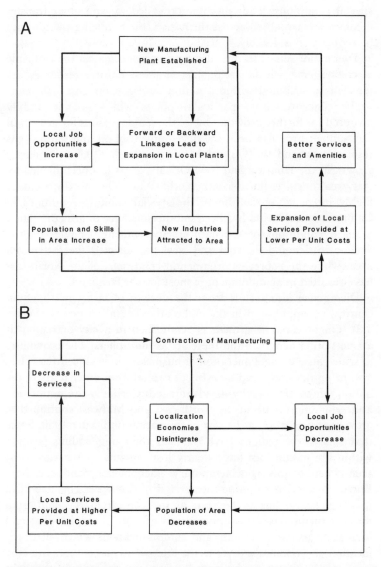

FIGURE 5.8 The process of cumulative causation (after Yeates 1980).
(A) The positive side: the economy of a region grows in response to cumulative causation and the multiplier effects of new factories and services.
(B) The negative side: factories close and have an impact on the total economy

special conditions: if the distribution of federal and other transfer incomes was equalised across the nation, the Sunbelt growth would be reduced considerably.

Two major sets of factors also tend to work against the principle of convergence within national economies: natural resources are unevenly distributed within a nation, and economic growth tends to be concentrated at particular points which become unduly favoured for further growth. One of the major reasons for growth in the Sunbelt area has been the development of oil and natural gas resources around the Gulf of Mexico since the 1930s. Economic growth in the Houston and New Orleans areas has been fuelled by this wealth since the Second World War. The development of highly intensive agriculture in the special climatic conditions of California and Florida has been another instance of growth related to local conditions of the natural environment. Conversely, the decline in demand for coal and steel has affected the Pittsburgh area, while the poorer environmental conditions of the North-east have resulted in abandonment of most former farmland.

Divergence also results from the growth of large metropolitan centres, as emphasised in the cumulative causation model (Figure 5.8). Once economic growth is established in a city or region, it attracts other activities and these act as multipliers. The economies of scale cause an agglomeration of businesses in such centres. They also bring in people and investment capital from other parts of the nation which are thereby disadvantaged. Certainly the population and economic wealth of the North-east and Midwest continued to grow at the expense of the rest of the nation until after 1950. Since that time these regions have retained their outstanding position within the nation, but have clearly lost impetus. It remains to be seen whether this is a temporary phenomenon, and the New England experience can be interpreted in this way. This aspect of divergence also has to be seen in the context of the shift from manufacturing-based to service-based growth in employment and increasing levels of mobility and communications which affect the location of economic activity in the late twentieth century. In many ways tendencies towards centralisation are changing – the light industries can be decentralised to peripheral areas, and many office jobs can be distributed more evenly throughout the nation. Such trends may enhance the convergence of socio-economic well-being, but it is too soon to draw firm conclusions.

5.3.3 Is it a matter of cyclic change?

Yet another view of the Sunbelt is that it has been a child of the economic conditions of the times seen in the context of cycles of growth and decline. The economist Walter Rostow (1977) has suggested that the model of economic change known as the 'Kondratieff Cycle' is relevant here. The cycle is characterised by the downswing in which manufacturing growth is encouraged by low raw material prices, low inflation and low interest rates, while raw-material-producing regions are at a disadvantage. In the subsequent upswing regions producing basic commodities obtain a better return, but this is to the detriment of manufacturing regions which experience recession due to a combination of higher prices, accelerated inflation and high interest rates. A general application of these cycles to the historical evolution of growth regions in the US can be made. The fifth of the cycles recognised in this way suggests that the Sunbelt phenomenon is related closely to the increase of energy and other commodity prices in the 1970s and a relative shift of advantage to raw material producers from the manufacturing regions. Since the cycle reversed its trend in the past when new resources were opened up and reduced the cost of food, materials and energy, the next swing to the advantage of manufacturers might be envisaged as occurring when the full benefits of applying automation to production are achieved. The (temporary?) swing to lower energy prices in 1986 provided a test of this idea:

> Economic growth in the oil states of Texas, Louisiana and Oklahoma had already started to slow down before this year's collapse in oil prices. Along with other states in the sunbelt, these three built their expansion during the 1970s not just on oil, but on manufacturing industries that have lately been in decline: cars, steel, chemicals, textiles. Then, in the 1980s, the rise of new service industries delivered some of the biggest gains in employment to America's north-east. As regional growth rates have converged since the beginning of this decade, many of the sunbelt states have seen net emigration, while parts of the frostbelt have had net immigration. Now, the oil-producing states, not yet used to being merely average, face their sternest economic test so far. (*Economist*, 8 March 1986)

This view encapsulated in the Kondratieff Cycle has been contested as too narrow in its outlook, since it focuses on the relationship of raw material production to wealth generated by manufacturing. Other costs such as labour and transport can be related to these, but also have separate factors impinging on them. Both are related to technological change, and the case for linking technological change to economic cycles is far from proven. In addition, the points already made about the shift out of manufacturing employment and into a growing importance accorded to amenity considerations suggest that economic cycles may be replaced by other forms of development control.

5.3.4 Is regional change controlled externally?

The location of economic activity, and its impact on other features of regional change, is subject to particular controls by those who determine the pattern of investment of capital. For much of the history of the United States this was essentially the province of individual entrepreneurs and later corporations. This factor has been put forward as the major reason for regional inequalities by those who champion a more centrally controlled economy. The control exercised by corporation headquarters in the national core region increased to the middle of the twentieth century, and often worked out in further growth within that part of the nation. However, it has been in the interests of such controllers to place new production units in other parts of the nation where there are lower labour costs. In addition, new economic activity has been generated outside the core.

Some of the reasons for a wider distribution of economic activity can be related to another 'control' factor: the increasing impact of government, and particularly Federal government, involvement in controlling the location of economic activity. This includes the siting of military bases and Federal institutions, but also the awarding of defence contracts and the provision of grant-aid for infrastructure to support economic development. The last of these has been responsible for much of the economic growth outside the national core region since 1950: the Inter-state Highway system, the network of regional and international airport facilities, water and sewerage, education and health facilities, to name a few of the areas of government involvement, have made it possible for economic growth to take place on a much wider basis than hitherto.

5.3.5 Does it reflect a deeper socio-economic change?

It has also been suggested that the Sunbelt development is part of the shift into the post-industrial society of the late twentieth century (Chapter 4). On this view the trends and patterns are seen as the products of the complex set of changes of value systems involved in the shift towards the post-industrial society. These changes involve demographic shifts related to changing views of marriage and the family; changing attitudes to employment and residential location; and a fundamental shift towards the South as the emerging manufacturing core of post-industrial America.

5.4 CONCLUSIONS

This survey and discussion has examined the 'Sunbelt' concept in relation to complementary changes in other parts of the nation. While the concept is valid in general terms, it requires more detailed consideration at the local level in both 'Sunbelt' and 'Frostbelt' areas, while some trends in the mid 1980s appear to be going against what has become characterised as a major trend in social and economic change within the United States. The intelligent observer will wish to assess whether this is a real trend or merely part of the 'boosterism' associated with many of the Sunbelt business leaders.

When it comes to explanations of these changes, there are many opinions, some of which take a narrowly economic view while others attempt a broader and sweeping overview. It is never easy to reach simple and final conclusions when one is in the midst of a set of critical changes, but such explanations are important for assessing the overall significance of trends in relation to future plans which affect the provision of services and the marketing of goods.

In terms of this study of regions and regionalism, the examination of the Sunbelt concept has highlighted the significance of both approaches – the descriptive and analytical results of regional comparisons within a nation, and the attitudes engendered by the generation of regional partisanship. To be most effective, the latter should be based on the former and not on purely emotional issues of a highly generalised nature.

6. Regions and Resources in the Late Twentieth Century: East v. West

6.1 INTRODUCTION

The Sunbelt–Frostbelt dichotomy is not the only example of regional differences becoming the basis for regionalistic attitudes in the US. There is also a growing set of differences between East and West. This has been exemplified by presidential elections since 1960, and the need to pick vice-presidential running-mates to provide a political base in other parts of the nation. Thus Kennedy (from New England) chose Johnson (from Texas); Johnson then chose Humphrey (Midwest); Nixon (California) chose Agnew (Virginia) and Ford (Midwest); Carter (Georgia) chose Mondale (Midwest). The importance of Reagan (California) choosing Bush was that the latter represented both Texas and his origins in New England, while neither Carter in 1976 and 1980 nor Mondale in 1984 covered the West.

Just as the Sunbelt represents elements across the southern margins of the US, so the East–West tension represents another set of differences within the nation. In this case, although the differences are less rooted in the history of the Civil War and subsequent denigration of the South, they result from another related situation – the evolution of the West out of a position of economic colonialism based on its own natural resources and the concentration of manufacturing in the East.

From the time when it was opened to settlement after the Civil War, the West was essentially a peripheral provider of raw materials to the core region of the US – firstly gold, followed by other metallic ores, then timber, fish, cattle and special farm crops.

It was also seen as a wilderness (with images enhanced by thousands of cowboy films), and large sections were preserved in the National Park system, while others were managed in a paternalistic fashion for the wider benefit of the nation as a whole. This type of image began to change earlier in the twentieth century, but the greatest shift took place during and after the Second World War. The metamorphosis of the West and its part in the nation can be related to a new economic outlook resulting from the development of intensive irrigation agriculture where there had been desert, the growth of major metropolitan centres on the west coast in particular, the discovery of major fuel resources in the 1970s at a time of energy shortages, and the increases in mobility afforded by jetplane and inter-state highway. This recent growth of the American West, its increasing role in the national consciousness, and its greater level of incorporation in the wider American economic system, are all related closely to issues of natural resource management: water, land and energy.

6.2 THE FUNDAMENTAL IMPORTANCE OF WATER RESOURCES

Most of the West is arid or semi-arid. The degree of aridity steadily increases after crossing the Mississippi from the east, and towards the south-west and, of all this vast area, only the northern parts of California and the coastal zones of Oregon and Washington have adequate rainfall.

Aridity is essentially a function of the relationship between inputs of rain, snow and other forms of precipitation on the one hand, and losses by evaporation and plant transpiration on the other. In Arizona low precipitation totals are combined with high evaporation and transpiration losses to produce an enormous difference between the two quantities. Farther north the evaporation factor is less in higher and colder terrain, but there is still an important gap not filled by precipitation. Rain falls on the California coast in winter, but the long dry summers effectively bring aridity to that section as well. Such shortfalls of water are reflected in the sparse desert vegetation, and were also responsible for the tiny numbers of amerinds which could be supported.

A very high proportion (often over 80 per cent) of the

precipitation which falls in the American West comes as snow deposited on the higher mountain ranges during winter months. This melts in spring and runs off in high-discharge floods over a few weeks. The economic development of the West in the twentieth century has depended for its impetus and continued expansion on the management of the natural availability of water. Massive sums of money have been invested to trap and store the flood waters to make them of use to farmers and urbanites through the rest of the year. Not only has water been made available over the whole year, but it has also been redistributed geographically from water-rich to water-poor sections of the West. This set of processes has affected many sectors of the socio-economic systems of the West, and has had impacts on the politics of the region.

The initial thrust for water resource development came from the East-dominated Federal government at the very beginning of the twentieth century. Although Senator Newlands of Nevada proposed the legislation, he was prompted to do so by those in Washington DC who felt that it was strategically important for the American West to be settled on a larger scale than had been possible up to that time: it was not sufficient for this region's economy to be based on the often ephemeral wealth obtained from its mines, and a more stable farming economy should be established and underwritten financially by the rest of the nation. The 1902 Newlands Reclamation Act paved the way for the modern developments in the West.

This Act provided funds for surveys and building of irrigation systems in the form of loans to be paid for by the sale of land which benefited from the provision of water. By the 1920s and 1930s dams were built to generate hydro-eletricity, as well as to store irrigation water, and during the economic depression the sale of electricity became the main source of income for repaying the Federal loans (since it was difficult to sell land). Water resources provided to farmers through the Bureau of Reclamation (a new agency within the Department of the Interior, established soon after the 1902 Act) thus passed on considerable subsidies, both in the form of initial low-interest loans and later as income from the sale of electricity. With cheap water available, the farmers of the West obtained significant cost advantages over those farther East by the mid twentieth century. They began by producing early-season vegetables and subtropical fruits which did not compete to a great extent with farmers in the East, but by the 1950s cotton-growing was moving rapidly out of the South to the irrigated areas (which were less troubled by plant diseases), and in the 1970s cattle-fattening was moving to feedlots in the south-west based on the irrigated production of fodder. The Bureau of Reclamation has thus played a major part in giving rise to the regional distinctiveness of the American West, and has attracted criticism for some of its impacts (Berkman and Viscusi, 1973).

Although the Federal water resource projects dominated the provision, more local schemes were also generated by city and state governments (California Water Atlas, 1977). Foremost among these were San Francisco and Los Angeles, although the city fathers of Salt Lake City probably had the longest history of such involvement. The importance of water to Los Angeles has been particularly great as the population in the metropolitan area has grown to 12.5 million, and illustrates the way in which water resources have affected socio-economic development in the West. Los Angeles is the largest city in the world established in a desert, but its growth has not been impeded by water shortages at any stage, largely due to the foresight of its managers in providing water ahead of demand. In the early years of the twentieth century Los Angeles seized the Owens Valley and built an aqueduct to take its water south to the city after removing the local farmers (by force when necessary). This water was too much for LA's own needs at the time, but brought with it considerable political power. In exchange for increased water supplies, many small towns in the Los Angeles basin agreed to merge with the city. Los Angeles was also involved in the establishment of the wider Metropolitan Water District in southern California, and for this a new aqueduct was built to bring water from the Colorado river. Although Los Angeles normally uses relatively small amounts of this more expensive water, it retains an important presence on its management body and was able to have access to the water in such times as the drought of 1976–7. Furthermore, the increasing political strength of Los Angeles in the State of California government assisted in the formulation of the State Water Project designed to bring water to the LA area from the wetter northern parts of the state.

San Francisco was also forced to obtain water from farther afield, and the need was made clear immediately after the 1906 earthquake. After much political manoeuvring, the city obtained permission to bring water from the Yosemite National Park, and the sale of this water within its own boundaries and to other neighbouring cities has resulted in San Francisco being able to run a range of other services without entry into the debts incurred in many American cities in recent years.

Throughout the West, economic development has been based on the availability of water resources. The provision has reached almost ridiculous levels at times: as in the bringing of water to lands of such great altitude that the growing season is too short to produce anything but grass and rapidly growing cereal crops which are over-produced elsewhere. The stability of agriculture supplied with cheap irrigation water has generated a set of settlement patterns and transport linkages throughout the West which are dependent on the continuing availability of water – and even on its increasing availability.

However, although water resources are renewable, they are not unlimited, and the limits of total water resources are now facing the West. The trend to go and find water from somewhere else has reached the end of the road, and ambitious projects such as the North America Water and Power Alliance (NAWAPA) are very unlikely to be implemented. Even the transfer of water from the Columbia river southwards has been excluded from discussion by measures passed in the US Congress in 1968 and confirmed again in 1978. Virtually all the major dams that can be built on the Colorado and other rivers of the West have already been built. Any further increase in demand for water will require a rearrangement of priorities, and these mean competition and raised emotions. Thus water resource provision is of particular importance in the West, and likely to become a major issue in the 1990s. Gone are the days when President Carter could turn down requests for Federal funds to be spent on water in the West on environmental grounds, or on the grounds of antagonism (i.e. lack of political support) from the East and its politicians dominating the US Congress. But this resource problem is one which creates an immediate difference in attitudes between easterner and westerner.

An example of the extent to which water has become fundamental to development in the West, and of the energies which can be invested in this aspect of natural resource usage, is the Central Arizona Project (Figure 6.1). This was envisaged first in the late 1940s (Johnson, 1977), since it was clear that the irrigation water

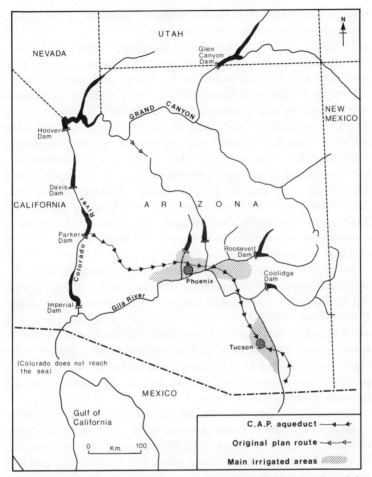

FIGURE 6.1   The Central Arizona Project. The aim of the project is to bring water from the River Colorado to the areas around Phoenix and Tucson

already provided for the areas around Phoenix and Tucson was going to be inadequate in the longer term. The building of the Roosevelt Dam (opened in 1911) and the Coolidge Dam (1927) by the Bureau of Reclamation had resulted in the extension of irrigation farming in the basinlands around these cities. However, the supply of water was more than matched by increasing demand for farming use, and farmers began to tap the underground water. In 1952 1 million acre-feet of water were drawn up in wells; this rose to 3 million (1960) and 4.6 million acre-feet in 1981. As a result, groundwater levels fall alarmingly.

In 1948 it had been proposed to bring water from the Colorado river to Central Arizona to make good this envisaged shortfall. It took 20 years to obtain legislation for this project, the delay being caused by a number of factors. Firstly, there were strong political objections from neighbouring states, particularly California. In the 1920s all the states in the Colorado basin – except Arizona – had signed a compact to share out the waters between them (and leaving a little over to flow into Mexico). Arizona had resisted this, but now had to request membership of the compact. This gave it 2.8 million acre-feet of the 15 million acre-feet which were considered available for extraction each year from the river on the basis of the pre-1920s flow records. But it took some years to convince the other states that Arizona should be admitted after its earlier intransigence.

Secondly, the proposals met environmental objections, since they envisaged taking water out of the Colorado where it flows across Arizona territory. This point was just downstream of the Grand Canyon and would have entailed building a storage dam with waters backing up into the lower section of the Canyon. Pressure was exerted by environmentalists to move the point of water extraction to Parker Dam, although this added to costs since more pumping power would be needed to take the water over and through intervening mountains.

Thirdly, it was realised that the annual flow of water down the Colorado had been reduced since the early 1920s estimates due to climatic changes. The State of California also made the point that Arizona already extracted 1 million acre-feet from the Salt and Gila rivers which are tributaries of the Colorado. So the amount which would be made available to Central Arizona was reduced from 2.8 to 1.8 million acre-feet. The fact that there was no Arizona State law to control the use of groundwater led to further debate over the project, and the Central Arizona Project legislation in 1968 demanded that such a system of control should be instituted before funds would be made available by the Federal government.

Even after the legislation was passed the project remained subject to varying levels of support in Washington, and its date of completion is now the late 1980s. In the period since 1968 extraction of groundwater has continued, and some places in

Arizona have had to face the issues imposed by limits on water resources. Thus the City of Tucson bought up surrounding farmland and took it out of production because there was insufficient water for both farmer and urbanite. This local clash foreshadows a major split of interests within the West – between the irrigation farmers who now constitute 2–3 per cent of the population but use 80–90 per cent of the water, and the people who live in metropolitan centres and are willing to pay more for their water. This debate has to be put into context: the farmers grumble that their water costs are rising and are making them uncompetitive with other producers, but this receives little sympathy farther east in areas where the farmers believe that the western irrigators have been favoured by cheap water costs for too long. Strong lobbies have been established by the western farmers and these will have the effect of raising the temperature of inter-regional debate on the water issue and will thus bring another regional issue to a warlike footing.

The East–West contrast was thus initiated by the natural distribution of water resources in the nation, and then enhanced by the policies adopted in attempts to even out the availability of water. In providing such financial assistance to the arid West, the Federal government did not expect that so much internal conflict would result.

6.3 LAND RESOURCES

The East–West differences, which are highlighted by the issue of water resources, are also closely related to contrasted views of land ownership and usage. In the East almost all the land is privately owned, and little is publicly held. If the Federal government wishes to establish a National Park, or National Forest, it has to buy the land from its previous owners (as in the Appalachians, Bradshaw, 1985). In the West most land is still owned by the Federal government, since individuals have not felt that it was worth purchasing arid mountainside.

Land use in the West is of low intensity outside the irrigated oases, due to the shortage of water and to other environmental limitations. The carrying capacity of much of this land is low, and expressed in terms of square miles per head of cattle. Vast tracts have not been purchased by private landowners, and are available

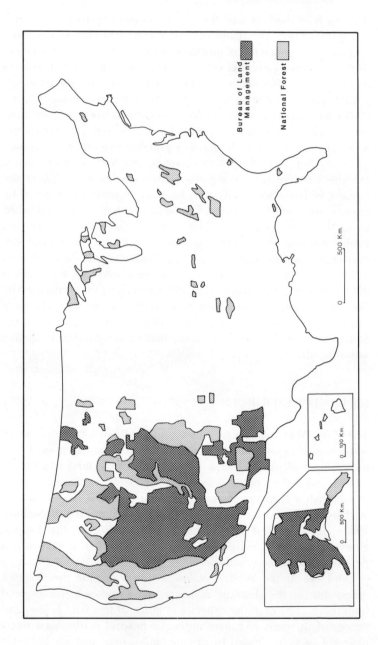

as pasture for rent through the Bureau of Land Management. Such rents have remained low, but increasing demands have been made on the pastures and groundwater levels have been lowered by nearby irrigation projects. The pastures have deteriorated in quality, but attempts by the government to improve them are costly, and the owners of the cattle do not have the money for increased rentals due to the falling returns from cattle farming. During the Carter administration, 1976–80, there was a major attempt by the Bureau to improve the condition of these upland pastures, but the increases in rentals generated what became known as the 'Sagebrush Revolution'. In the West this was linked to the administration's reluctance to provide more funds for water resource provision, and played an important part in generating antagonism towards the Carter administration and in gaining sympathy for the Reagan cause. Since he has been in office, President Reagan has supported water resource projects again, and has not been so interested in environmental conservation.

In addition to these grazing lands, the Federal government also holds other huge tracts of land in the West (Figure 6.2). They include most of the wilderness lands, National Parks and National Forests, together with extensive areas of military lands for testing weapons and space vehicles. The restrictive land uses which are possible within the boundaries of such Federal land are often cited as a factor preventing other types of productive land use and employment for local people. There is a resentment in the West, due to this type of Federal presence and the fact that so much land in each state is seen as being controlled from Washington DC on the east coast. This resentment tends to give rise to anti-government attitudes and many of the anti-tax and states-rights movements of recent years have originated in this part of the US.

The most intense land battles of recent years have been fought in Alaska. Many of the issues which emerged there have been taken up elsewhere. The State of Alaska is separated from the rest of the US, and has a tiny population in a huge area, but has been subject to a three-way tug of war over the ownership of land since it

FIGURE 6.2 Lands owned by two US Federal agencies: the National Forest Service and the Bureau of Land Management. In addition, the National Park Service also owns much land which is mainly in the West (after Bennett, 1983)

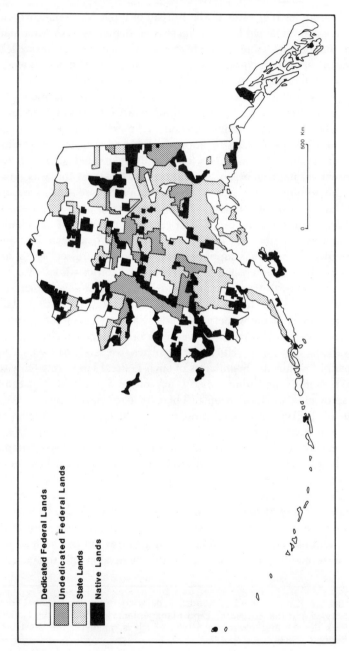

became a fully-fledged state in 1959. At that stage the Federal government still controlled over 99 per cent of Alaskan lands, and undertook to transfer nearly a third of this to the new state.

The issues were brought to a head in the 1960s, when it was discovered that Alaska possessed major oil resources. The environmental lobby in the rest of the US objected to the economic exploitation of America's 'last wilderness'; the State of Alaska wanted to encourage as much economic development as possible; and the aboriginal peoples (amerinds, nunumiats and aleuts) began to make the case that they also had rights to the land and were willing to fight for them in the courts. Throughout the 1970s a debate raged as to which constituency should have most of its way, and during the Carter administration the native and environmental interests appeared to be winning. By the end of 1980, following the election of President Reagan, a rapid compromise was reached by the US Congress in which the aboriginal peoples were allotted considerable areas, the State of Alaska was allowed to encourage economic development over a third of the territory, and sections were tied up in large Wilderness Areas and National Parks (Figure 6.3). The sections removed from the possibility of future economic development were not as large as the environmentalists had hoped, but some final decisions were left open for another five years so that a more thorough assessment of mineral resources could be made (Lynch et al., 1981).

The farmland which is owned privately in the West is often subject to different rules from those affecting land in the East. Thus, in California there are often much larger holdings than those of the typical family farms in the East. Although most of the former Spanish/Mexican haciendas were broken up and sold off as small irrigation farms in the late nineteenth and early twentieth centuries, there are still large holdings which arose out of land grants by the Federal government to railroad companies in the late nineteenth century. The Southern Pacific Railroad Company is one of the largest landowners in California, and has several extensive holdings which are also irrigated by government projects – despite the rules limiting the acreage which can be used in this way. Such large land-holdings have made it difficult to apply the water resource

FIGURE 6.3   Land ownership in Alaska, 1980 (after Epps)

allocations allowed by Federal legislation in many parts of California, and the wealth resulting from the farming of these lands has provided a basis of political power for some of the families concerned (Fellmeth, 1973).

The distinctive patterns of land ownership in the West have both fuelled continuing resentment against the Federal government and have provided a base of political power in conjunction with water rights and cheap subsidised water for irrigation. This combination has also resulted in attitudes in the West which those in the East find it difficult to understand.

6.4 THE CHANGING PATTERN OF ENERGY RESOURCE PROVISION

If the use of water and land resources are fundamental to an understanding of the growing rift between East and West within the United States, the shift in energy production is also having major repercussions. Energy considerations are also both national and regional in their implications. The United States is the world's most affluent nation, and this affluence is based on an increasing use of energy resources. Up to 1950 it could be self-sufficient in coal, oil and natural gas, but with the move to greater use of oil (rather than coal) domestic production became insufficient and it began to import cheap oil from the Middle East. The growing economic dominance of the US took up 40 per cent of the world's energy supplies in 1960. Although this dominance is now reduced, due to the growth of demand in other urban-industrial nations, energy considerations are still of great importance for the US.

The rising costs of imported oil, enhanced suddenly by the crises of 1973 and 1979, brought problems of energy shortages and inflation. President Carter saw national energy policy as a major issue, and attempted to institute a unified approach. Although this did not succeed, the market changes in the mid 1970s led to increased internal oil production and also to a shift back to coal-mining: total US production of coal was projected to double from 600 million tons in 1970 to over 1200 million tons by 1980. This has not been achieved, but output reached a high of 838 million tons in 1982, followed by a reduction due to economic recession and other factors which reduced demand at home and abroad. At the same time, investment was made in alternative energy sources, and particularly in nuclear electricity plants. Massive expansion in the number of US nuclear power plants took place in the early 1970s, but progress was slowed by the Three Mile Island incident. Research took place for a while into other sources of fuels, such as oil shale, and into energy sources such as solar radiation, wind and waves, but falling oil prices in the mid 1980s have led to the reduction of such work. Furthermore, conservation programmes have been successful, particularly in energy-poor regions such as New England, and demand for energy resources has not risen as expected.

The main results of the 'energy crisis' of the 1970s have been the increase of coal production and the search for new oil deposits. Both have had an impact on parts of the West, and have brought them to greater national prominence. This is also related to the parallel development of environmental legislation for air quality, which has placed nationwide penalties on the burning of coal with a high sulphur content. The major coal-mining area of the US up to 1970 was the Appalachian Mountains from Pennsylvania to Alabama. Some mining also extended beneath the Midwest plains of Indiana and Illinois. But most of this coal had a high sulphur content and was not subject to such major increases in production in the 1970s as the mining areas with low sulphur content. Only eastern Kentucky and southern West Virginia of the Appalachian and Midwest fields had coals with low sulphur content, and these areas experienced the expansion of mining in the established eastern areas. But new coalfields were also developed in the 1970s in the West. In 1970 only 6 million tons of coal were produced in Wyoming, up from 5 million tons in 1950, but by 1983 this had risen to 112 million tons. Wyoming coal production equalled that of West Virginia by 1983, and was only a little behind Kentucky. This shift involved the construction of new railroad lines, the inmigration of people to work in the mines (Wyoming's small population grew by 41 per cent in the 1970s), and the construction of new housing and service provision in a formerly sparsely populated state. The surface extraction of coal on such a large scale made major demands on landscape and water supplies, and left much of the surface in a state which can only be described as desertification.

Other aspects of energy development in the West focus on the discovery of new oil deposits, as in the Overthrust Belt of the central Rockies where there has been a rapid expansion of exploration and production. Oil is also available to the west coast in large quantities from the Alaskan fields, which were discovered in the 1960s and were delivering oil on a major scale by the late 1970s. Most of the US uranium production is also concentrated in this region, together with the largest proportion of hydro-electricity generation. For the future, the sunny West has greater prospects for solar power, and the major oil shale deposits of the nation are found in Colorado.

This places a greater gulf between the East and the West of the United States. Up to the 1970s the East still dominated the production of coal and had easiest access to the cheap oil from the Middle East. That has all changed.

6.5 THE ROLE OF OTHER NATURAL RESOURCES

Other natural resources may be less significant in the differentiation of East and West in terms of their overall impact on the economy, but add further distinctiveness. The West dominates the production of non-ferrous metal ores from gold to copper and the steel alloy additives (molybdenum, manganese). Throughout the twentieth century it has been the main source of constructional timber, although the south-east has become increasingly important for timber for paper, pulp and chemical products. And the West has also been a major source of tinned fish products, particularly salmon and tuna.

The eastern part of the US, after using its own local resources, has become an increasing user of those from other parts of the nation and world. Its former primary industries of fishing, farming, mining and timber-production were reduced in significance by the early twentieth century, at least in terms of the proportion of workers employed. Thus, the East became the manufacturing workshop and the financial and political control centre of the US, and other regions felt they were subordinate to, and were even being exploited by, the easterners. This pattern of economic colonialism has changed since 1950, but it can still generate emotive issues.

6.6 THE AMENITY FACTOR

Just as this factor was important in the Sunbelt–Frostbelt tension, so it has assumed increasing significance in the West. The West always contained the most dramatic terrains within the borders of the United States, and this fact is reflected in the number of National Parks and Wilderness Areas designated there. The increased mobility of people since the Second World War – both in terms of transport systems and financially – has emphasised the importance of these scenic wonders for increased tourism, and also the pleasantness of western environments for residential location. The combination of National Parks, mountains with increasing facilities for winter sports and summer trekking, artificial lakes with watersport activities, and the distinctive desert and coastal environments, has attracted increasing numbers of tourists and inmigrants. The latter come both for the growing numbers of jobs and also as retirees.

The US West has acquired a new image as a growth area in its own right since the 1950s, and has experienced high rates of population growth since 1970. Many eastern Americans view Denver, and the other cities lying at the foot of the Rockies, as a haven they would like to reside in. The combination of high-income jobs and access to varied recreation opportunities in this area has been potent.

6.7 CONCLUSIONS

Any conflict between East and West may be some years in the future, but the basic differences are already in place and the issues resulting from them are affecting political attitudes and activities. Once again, the regional differences are giving rise to the stances of regionalism.

People living in the West resent what they see as control and exploitation by the East of their local natural resources such as water, land and minerals. In the past this has resulted in removal of much of the wealth to the East and to the bank accounts of investors in mining and timber companies. Those living in the East view such attitudes as ungrateful, since the cheap irrigation water is largely produced by courtesy of eastern subsidies. They also resent the fact that it has been used in unfair competition to the detriment of eastern farmers in the former Cotton Belt and in the meat-producing region of the Midwest: cheap water has allowed western farmers to grow fodder for the expanding feedlot concentrations of animal products.

However, these attitudes may be passing. The former colonial relationship between East and West is changing as new urban-industrial centres such as Los Angeles, the San Francisco Bay Area, Seattle, Denver and Phoenix, provide a more complex set of inter-relationships between East and West and within the West. This illustrates the fact that regionalism my be engendered by temporary sets of attitudes.

7. Changes in the Urban-industrial Economy: Poverty and Affluence

7.1 INTRODUCTION

Regional differences within the United States are not merely a matter of North–South or East–West, historical territorial antagonisms or resource availability. A sort of regionalism has been generated by contrasts of socio-economic well-being within the nation – what has been called the 'geography of poverty'. The convergence of both incomes and access to mobility and services across the US has tended to mask major variations in economic and social conditions. Up to 1970 these variations were reflected in growing urban–rural contrasts, and particularly in those at the metropolitan–rural level, resulting in urban affluence and rural poverty. Since the mid 1960s these contrasts have been evened out to an extent, but there has been a shift in the concentration of poverty to inner city locations. This shift has changed the scale of regional consideration, and reflects major changes in American society.

7.2 THE ERA OF RURAL POVERTY

Throughout the twentieth century there has been a trend of population movement from rural areas to the cities of America. In 1920 those living in urban places exceeded the numbers in rural areas for the first time; by 1970 two-thirds of the US population were living in metropolitan centres. This trend reflected the shift from farm employment and life in rural communities to employment

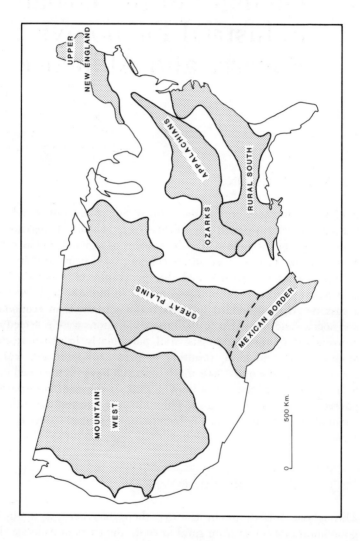

firstly in manufacturing and later in urban-based service industries. The whole process has had such major economic and social impacts that it has formed the subject matter of many novels and films.

A 1970 study of poverty in the US (Morrill and Wohlenberg) emphasised the rural location of the poor (Figure 7.1). At this stage poverty could be related to conditions of education, unemployment, elderly age groups and race. On the basis of these conditions, poverty rates in non-metropolitan regions were twice those in metropolitan, although the actual numbers of poor were approximately equal due to the greater total of people who lived in large cities. Studies of the distribution of poverty by states showed that groups of rural states had a higher incidence than states with large urban populations. Another study which compared the richest and poorest counties in the US in 1970 (Guinness and Bradshaw, 1985) also emphasised the contrast between suburban metropolitan counties and the rural counties of the coastal and Appalachian South.

The Morrill–Wohlenberg study showed that poverty in the US in 1970 was partly a matter of economic conditions. These included access to jobs, and particularly those which paid well. Such access was related partly to the policies of firms in the siting of employment opportunities, and was partly a matter of the willingness of people to move to places where such opportunities were being created. In many rural areas there was the combination of a dearth of new jobs and a reluctance to move to other places where conditions were better. At this time, rural areas underwent a major reduction of the jobs in traditional rural industries – farming, mining, forestry – and related services. The alternative to those who insisted on remaining in the rural locations was often low-wage manufacturing. Thus rural areas across the US, together with urban centres in the South and other urban centres in regions of economic decline (e.g. New England at the time), were characterised by high unemployment as a result of the lag between one phase of economic activity and the next. They were also characterised by high levels of underemployment and dependent population (i.e. those too old or too young to work). Thus the per capita incomes were much lower than in economic growth regions (mainly metropolitan centres at

FIGURE 7.1 The poverty regions of the US in the 1960s (after Morrill and Wohlenburg, 1971). These are all rural areas

this stage), and family incomes were also lower due to the lack of second incomes.

Such economic conditions, involving supply and demand, had to be seen in the context of social conditions at the time. These included factors such as education, age, family structure and race. Thus, low incomes were associated with those having poorer education, the retired sector, large family size or single-parent families, and with black or Hispanic race.

When both economic and social characteristics were combined, the rural–urban contrast stood out since those living in rural areas had fewer chances of access to new jobs as traditional ones declined, were often more poorly educated and belonged to larger families. The poorest areas of all in the US were those in Atlantic and Gulf coastal plains of the rural South, where the dominantly black population was even further disadvantaged. The declining coalfield areas of central Appalachia, with a largely white population, were not far in advance of the worst areas.

Over the period 1950 to 1970 there had been a shift from the rural areas towards the inner cities, but in 1970 the rurally-located poverty still involved half the poor population of the US and affected three-quarters of the national area. Such contrasts between rural and metropolitan conditions provided a basis for different types of Federal government action in both the 1930s and the mid 1960s. This is the theme of Chapters 8 to 10. Rural poverty has decreased as the result of a combination of Federal grant-aid and welfare assistance, the improvement of access to major centres of economic activity, the spread of manufacturing and service employment into rural areas, and the movement of people with higher incomes from the largest cities into rural places.

7.3 THE ERA OF INNER URBAN POVERTY

During the late 1960s and 1970s the numbers of Americans below the poverty line decreased from 40,000,000 in 1960 to under 25,000,000 (from 22.4 to under 12 per cent of total population), a figure maintained from 1970 to 1978 (Figure 7.2). At the same time the location of the worst concentrations of poverty moved from rural areas to inner cities (Figure 7.3). Whereas poverty had been concentrated in rural areas in 1959 (also reflected in a high

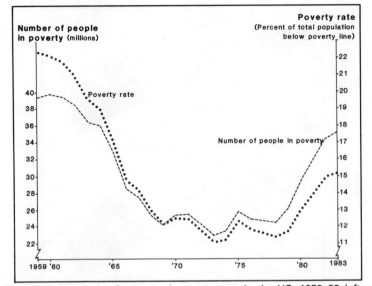

FIGURE 7.2 Numbers of poor, and poverty rate, in the US, 1959–83 (after O'Hare, 1985)

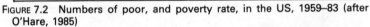

	Number of poor(1,000s)			Poverty rate(percent)		
Area	1959	1978	1983	1959	1978	1983
Total	38,766	24,497	35,266	22.0	11.4	15.2
REGIONS						
South	19,116	10,255	13,484	35.4	14.7	17.2
Outside the South	19,650	14,242	21,782	16.0	9.8	14.2
Northeast		5,050	6,561		10.4	13.4
North Central		5,192			9.1	14.6
West		4,000	6,684		10.0	14.7
NONMETROPOLITAN AND METROPOLITAN AREAS						
Nonmetropolitan areas	21,747	9,407	13,516	33.2	13.5	18.3
Metropolitan areas	17,019	15,090	21,750	15.3	10.4	13.8
Central cities	10,437	9,285	12,872	18.3	15.4	19.8
Suburbs	6,582	5,805	8,878	12.2	6.8	9.6

FIGURE 7.3 The regional nature of poverty in the US, 1959, 1978 and 1983 (after O'Hare, 1985)

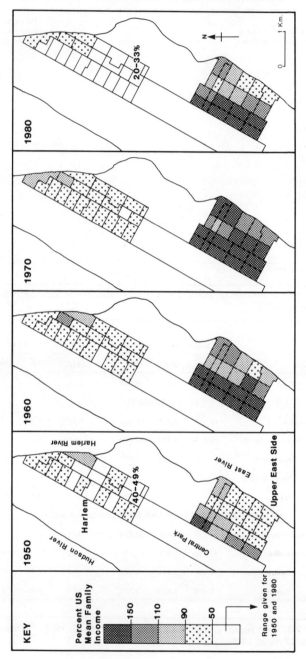

incidence in the South), by 1978 the inner city poverty rate exceeded that of rural areas. This was a period when Federal assistance was made available on a large scale to rural areas, and also when the climax was reached in the 1920s–1960s migration of blacks and Hispanics to the inner city areas of the major metropolitan centres.

After 1978 poverty levels in the US began to rise again due to economic recession and, after Reagan's election, the reduction of government programmes to assist poverty. But the inner city poverty rate remained above the rural rate. Thus, the inner cities have replaced the rural areas as the main poverty-stricken areas in the US. Many of them consist of the 'left-behind' element of the 1980s, just as the rural areas contained large numbers of the 'left-behind' element resulting from the socio-economic events of mid century. In the most difficult areas the black middle class generated by access to government jobs has followed the white middle class in moving out of the inner city. This has given rise to 'expanded ghettos' in areas of better housing, often adjacent to the original ghetto, but where the economic conditions of black families are greatly improved. There has been some limited development of outer suburbs as the homes of black families. These movements have also resulted in the worsening of conditions in the older ghettos: the Harlem district of central New York and the inner black ghetto of Chicago have deteriorated in socio-economic conditions compared to US norms between 1950 and 1980. The reduction in the numbers of black people moving into these older ghetto areas from the South since the 1960s, combined with the loss of the more affluent black families, has resulted in the abandonment of property and the decline of services (Figure 7.4).

There is talk of 'a nation apart', and 'a new underclass' (US News & World Report, 17 March 1986), to describe what appears to be an intractable problem of the 'left-behind' inner city minority poor. The problem involves long-term unemployment, broken homes, dilapidated housing, welfare-dependence, and often drugs and violence. It was estimated in 1986 to affect between 2 and 3.5 million people, nearly all blacks in inner cities.

FIGURE 7.4 The increasing poverty of the black inner-city area of Harlem, New York, 1950–80. These maps are based on US Bureau of Census data at the census tract level

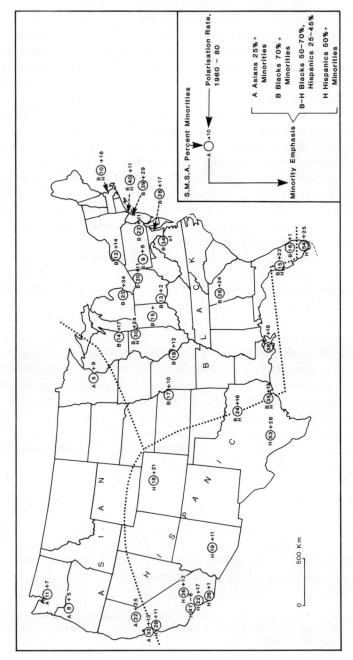

This inner city poverty also has a marked regional dimension, since it is most obvious in the cities of the North-east and Midwest which attracted the largest number of black migrants from the South between 1940 and 1960: New York, Philadelphia, Baltimore, Washington DC, Pittsburgh, Cleveland, Detroit and Chicago. These 'Frostbelt' cities are those where manufacturing employment is declining, and most new jobs have been created in suburban areas. Almost all jobs in inner city areas are either high-paid (requiring high education), or low-paid and often part-time.

The problem of the black ghettos exists elsewhere in the US, but is not so obvious: the cities of the Great Plains and north-west have low percentages of black people; the Sunbelt cities also have somewhat smaller black populations and more new jobs, while there is often less of a trapped ghetto feeling in many of them. Thus, although residential segregation is still high in cities such as Atlanta, most blacks live in an expanding sector to the west of the city centre. Those with upward economic mobility can move into black suburban areas, living in ranch-style houses and enjoying many of the conditions available to affluent whites. In the San Francisco Bay area on the west coast, groups of blacks live in a number of small locations around the Bay, rather than in a single embattled area. Los Angeles has a larger proportion of blacks in its population than other cities of the West, but the housing conditions are very different from the old worker housing of north-eastern cities, and there are also wealthy black districts.

A recent study by Winsburg (1986) has demonstrated that these major American cities have increased their proportion of the minority populations (and thus of poverty) since 1960. In the twenty years to 1980 the proportion of minority populations in the 38 largest metropolitan areas in the US rose from 42 to 51 per cent of the total populations. Since most minority groups have lower incomes than the non-Hispanic white majority, this confirms the increasing concentration of poverty in major urban areas.

This study has also shown that there is a strong regional component to the distribution of minorities (Figure 7.5). Four types are recognised:

FIGURE 7.5 The proportion of minorities in the largest metropolitan areas of the US. There is a distinctive regional emphasis and different levels of polarisation between the minority populations of inner and outer cities (after Winsburg, 1986)

(1) The largest group of 18 metropolitan areas has blacks forming 70 per cent and more of the minority population. All but 3 of these metropolitan areas are in the Manufacturing Belt area of the North-east and Midwest regions, where the total minority populations range 13–20 per cent in the Midwest and 22–34 per cent in the strip between New Jersey and Washington. Pittsburgh has the lowest minority population in this group (9 per cent).

The other three cities dominated by black minorities are in the South: Atlanta, New Orleans and Fort Lauderdale.

(2) Hispanics are the second minority group in the US, and may become the largest by AD 2000. Nine cities have Hispanics forming 50 per cent or more of the total minority populations. These are all in the south-west, and mostly close to the Mexican border. Miami is the important exception with 54 per cent of its total population composed of minorities. These Hispanic metropolitan areas as a whole have higher minority populations than the black metro areas.

(3) Six metropolitan areas have black populations making up 50–70 per cent, and Hispanics 25–45 per cent, of the minority total. These include the two largest metropolitan areas of the North, New York and Chicago (with total minority proportions of 40 and 30 per cent respectively), and Boston which has a smaller total of minorities. The other three such metro areas occur on the borders between the old South and the Hispanic zone.

(4) Asians are seldom a dominant minority group, but they make up more than 25 per cent of the minority population in five of the largest metropolitan areas. These are mainly on the west coast and outside the main Hispanic influence, but also include Minneapolis, which has the lowest minority proportion of all these 38 metro areas.

Winsburg's study also showed that there had been increasing polarisation between the inner city and outer city areas of these metropolitan centres between 1960 and 1980. The polarisation was measured as the difference in percentage of non-Hispanic whites in the total populations between the central city and outer city. The rate of polarisation is the change between 1960 and 1980. Only one city of the 38, Los Angeles, recorded a lower polarisation in 1980 than in 1960, but this was because the non-Hispanic white population of both its central city and outer city declined rapidly – by 29 and 35 per cent of the total populations respectively. In other metropolitan areas the declining proportions of non-Hispanic whites were much lower in the outer than the central cities, and so rates of polarisation increased.

The outcome of this study is to emphasise the large and growing minority (and low-income) groups in the major metropolitan areas, but also to show that the situation varies across the US in terms of its magnitude and nature.

Inner city poverty is a phenomenon which has grown to become the major reflection of unequal opportunity and achievement in the United States of the 1970s and 1980s. It exhibits many of the features of the earlier rural poverty: left-behind groups unable to gain access to employment and unable to move elsewhere in many cases. Although not strictly a 'regional' problem in terms of geographical scale in each city, it can be viewed as an important spatial disharmony which can be considered with those at the larger subnational and national scales. It might also be said that it does have a regional dimension which is partly tied up with the Sunbelt–Frostbelt problem. And, like many of the regional problems discussed so far, it provides the basis for locally-based activism and political lobbies.

7.4 MAJOR URBAN REGIONS

While the shift between rural and inner city poverty has been taking place, the dominance of metropolitan centres as places of residence and work has resulted in the new concept of metropolitan regions referred to in Chapter 1. A series of large metropolitan centres, each often containing over a million people, has become the economic focus of the surrounding areas, rather than older region-defining characteristics such as natural features and resources. Instead of a region being defined by its outer boundary, it has become functionally based on links with the central metropolitan base.

In some parts of the US, where such metropolitan centres are close to each other, interactions between two or several have increased to the point where they can almost be regarded as a

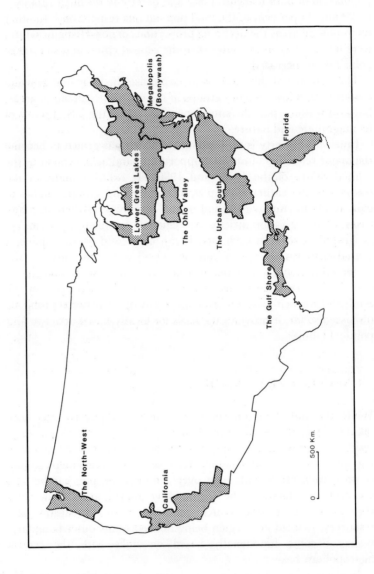

single functioning entity. This phenomenon gave rise to the concept of 'Megalopolis' (Gottman, 1961) in the late 1950s, and to that of the 'Major Urban Region' (Yeates, 1980). Gottman's Megalopolis referred to the still-unique conglomeration of metropolitan centres on the north-eastern seaboard from Boston to Washington DC (often called 'Boswash', or 'Bosnywash'). These cities had been sited close to each other in the colonial era, and their growth had been maintained due to promotion stimulated by competition between their states in the nineteenth century. By the middle of the twentieth century they provided an almost continuous built-up environment, although half of the area covered was wooded. Even in the wooded area outside and between the major urban areas, the most important economic activities supporting the population were those focused on the functioning of the major cities. Farming produce was directed towards the huge city markets, many people living in the outer suburbs and 'exurbs' worked in the city centres or suburbs, and remaining rural areas were devoted to recreation functions to serve the populations of the cities.

Although Megalopolis remained unique in its concentration of some 40 million people, and in the sheer scale of its activities, other groupings of metropolitan centres also began to be identified as functioning and growing together (Figure 7.6) by the 1970s. This served further to emphasise the importance of the metropolitan phenomenon. Within these Major Urban Regions of North America, distinctions can be drawn on the basis of their position within the US. The MURs of Bosnywash and the Great Lakes share a history of manufacturing development and economic growth in the late nineteenth century and up to the 1950s. They are therefore characterised by extensive tracts of large factories and attendant infrastructure, older worker housing, fragmented political jurisdictions, and the greatest degree of outer suburb v. inner city tensions. The MURs of the South and West have similar social problems, but often in less concentrated form, have a newer built environment dominated by expansion since 1945, and often have more effective overall political control of the major part of the urbanised areas.

FIGURE 7.6   The major urban regions of the US (after Yeates, 1980)

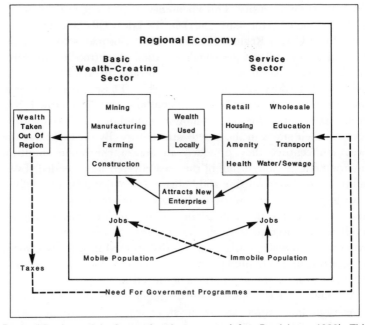

FIGURE 7.7   A model of a regional economy (after Bradshaw, 1982). This links the internal generation of wealth with economic colonialism and the role of national public policies

7.5 CONCLUSIONS

It is thus clear that there has been a major shift in poverty from the rural areas of the US in the 1950s and 1960s to the inner cities in the 1970s and 1980s. This movement has changed the patterns of regional need by concentrating the deprived population in the smaller areas of inner-city ghettos. In each case the location of concentrations of poverty is the result of a lag in the ability of the free market economy to adjust to major changes imposed on it. This has led to widespread distress among large sections of the American population, and the governments at these times have perceived a need to try and help those who have been disadvantaged by this slow process of adjustment (Figure 7.7). There have been attempts to make Federal funding available to rural areas, and then to switch resources back from rural-based programmes to the inner-urban areas to deal with the attendant problems. However, although the rural programmes had some successes, the size of the urban problems has defeated attempts to alleviate them to date. These programmes are discussed more fully in Chapters 8 to 10.

This aspect of American geography also serves to further emphasise the importance of the regional dimension. Not all large cities are the same, and different minority groups have different needs and attitudes to their situation. There is a distinct regional element to the geographical arrangement of these characteristics. The Asian groups tend to be most able to take advantage of the opportunities in the US system for economic improvement, and as many move to the suburbs as arrive as new immigrants. Hispanics are also moving to the suburbs, but at a slower rate, while the blacks lag behind to the greatest extent in such movements. These differences are important in any responses to the pressures for assistance with the problems of the disadvantaged minority groups in inner cities.

8. Public Policy and Regionalism: I. Tennessee Valley Authority

8.1 INTRODUCTION

The discussion of regionalism so far in this book has referred to informal processes – the generation of regional feelings leading to their expression in the pressures impinging on the political arena. There is also a more formal aspect to the development of regionalism in the United States through the medium of public policy. This has taken its cue from the expression of feelings engendered by regional inequalities of well-being, and has resulted in a number of attempts to legislate for regional improvements. While Federal legislation has had regional impacts on water resources, land use and energy production, and has also indirectly affected regional economic development through such measures as the Inter-state Highway programme, it has become involved in a smaller way with specific regional development programmes.

Such attempts at regional economic development have started with a particular disadvantage in the US. The Federal Constitution recognises only two units – the Federal government and state governments – while regional units tend to involve parts of several states. This has the result that any regional authorities brought into being by Federal legislation require powers to override state interests if they are not to become subject to those interests. A similar problem has faced plans which involve groupings of counties for the purpose of local economic development: not only have these plans overridden established political units of decision-making (counties and municipalities), but they are also confined within state boundaries, even although some local planning might be best carried out across a state border. Such constitutional issues can always be guaranteed to provide discussion in the United States.

In addition to the stability of established internal boundaries, the US political environment is characterised by its conservatism. This is often expressed in a reluctance to plan for any form of economic development through public policies. Such attitudes are based on the assumption that economic development is best left to private enterprise rather than government bureaucrats. This dominant conservatism has restricted Federal intervention, which is based on more liberal attitudes, to three short periods of a year or so each in the twentieth century, and a regional dimension to public policy has been involved in only two.

The first phase of intervention occurred in the early years of the twentieth century, when conservationist views were important to President Theodore Roosevelt. The water resources legislation, and the Forest Service and Parks Service, were established in this phase, at least in general principle, but there were no region-specific programmes. The second phase occurred in the first year or so of President Franklin Roosevelt's 'New Deal' administration beginning in January 1933. At this time the economic depression was at its worst, and there were widespread demands for government intervention. Roosevelt established a National Planning Board in 1933 (changed to National Resources Committee in 1935), and encouraged states to create their own plans for funding by the Federal government. One of the major projects which resulted was the establishment of the Tennessee Valley Authority, touted as the start of a nationwide process of regional development. TVA remained a one-off, although some of its characteristics were repeated in the Columbia River Basin of the Pacific north-west. Much of what it accomplished in the Tennessee Valley – as opposed to views of what was intended – has been carried out elsewhere by the US Army Corps of Engineers. Further developments along the lines of river basin planning were deferred by the Second World War and the growing feeling that such planning was 'socialist'. The concept of national planning was not resurrected after this (Wilson, 1980).

A third phase of Federal intervention was instituted with the

Kennedy administration of the early 1960s, but little was achieved until the Johnson 'Great Society' era of the mid 1960s. Once again, a year of so of intense interventionist legislation was followed by years when conservatism reigned during the 1970s and 1980s. During this period a number of other region-based programmes were instigated, although they formed a small proportion of the total range of Federal programmes available to the nation.

The next three chapters are devoted to a consideration of federally sponsored regionalism in relation to the specific programmes instituted in the 1930s and the 1960s. These are: the Tennessee Valley Authority (established 1933); the Area Redevelopment Administration (1961); the Appalachian Regional Commission (1965); the Economic Development Administration and the 'Title V' Regional Commissions (established as part of the Public Works and Economic Development Act of 1965) within the Department of Commerce; and a number of river basin commissions (established by the Water Resources Act of 1965). These agencies are evaluated in terms of the sources of regional attitudes and pressures, the contemporary political possibilities, and also the state of thinking at the time concerning regional economic development. Their relative success is assessed in terms of the ways in which they have, or have not, fulfilled their legislative remits, and have, or have not, been able to broaden the concept of public regionalism.

8.2 THE TENNESSEE VALLEY AUTHORITY: ITS BEGINNINGS

When Franklin Roosevelt was installed as president of the United States at the beginning of 1933, he needed to act quickly to demonstrate that the Federal government could achieve something to help the lot of so many Americans who had been put out of work by the economic depression. One of the first programmes to be established was that which set up the Tennessee Valley Authority on 18 May 1933. Its legislative remit appears rather prosaic:

> to improve the navigability and to provide for the flood control of the Tennessee river; to provide for reforestation and proper use of marginal lands in the Tennessee Valley; to provide for the

agricultural and industrial development of said valley; to provide for the national defense by the creation of a corporation for the operation of Government properties at and near Muscle Shoals in the State of Alabama, and for other purposes.

However, this programme combined many of the elements Roosevelt wished to use to demonstrate what government planning could achieve. The hills of southern Appalachia were inhabited by poor white farmers having average family incomes of less than 45 per cent of the US norm, and were perceived as being in need of outside assistance. The region suffered from severe soil erosion due to the combination of steep slopes and out-dated farming methods. It also lacked alternative employment prospects, while economic development was retarded by high electricity prices and poor provision for transport, health-care, education and water/sewer facilities (Bradshaw, 1984a).

During the 1920s a number of idealists in the Regional Planning Association of America had been proposing that the government should plan for the social and economic development of rural areas, and so reduce the effects of the expansion of the unhealthy and overcrowded urban-industrial centres of the North (Friedmann and Weaver, 1979). Some of these ideas had centred around the river basin as a unit for organising integrated regional development, and had been adopted by a number of the early sponsors of the TVA project. Perhaps more relevant for the quick start required by Roosevelt in 1933 was the fact that the US Army Corps of Engineers had already prepared plans for controlling flooding along all tributaries of the Mississippi after disastrous inundations in the mid 1920s. Also, a number of detailed plans for building reservoir dams were available from the Bureau of Reclamation, which had constructed several in the far West of the US.

The choice of the Tennessee basin (rather than a number of other contenders, such as the neighbouring Cumberland) was made for the reason that it also enabled Roosevelt to tidy up the debate over the use of the former munitions plant at Muscle Shoals in northern Alabama. This, and the related hydroelectric power plant at Wilson Dam, had been built during the First World War.

Thus, the political need and opportunity for action, the means of dealing with the problem, and practical technological and political factors, all came together at this time and place. Roosevelt could

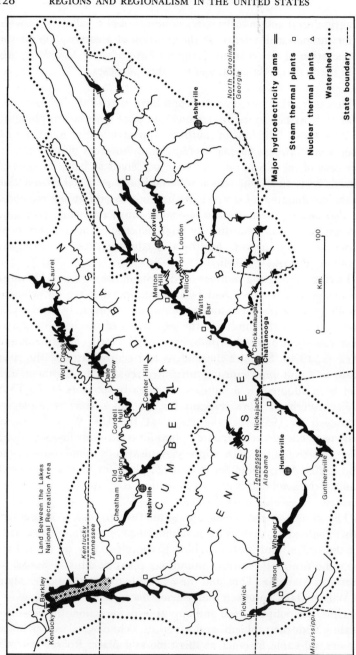

also appreciate this type of plan, since he had been involved with similar resource-use planning as Governor of New York. His close advisers could also discern a broader prospect of such planning being applied across the nation: they envisaged economic and social growth on a large and extending scale. TVA was only a beginning.

8.3 TVA: THE FORMATIVE YEARS

Within three months of the legislation being signed into being by the president, the construction of Norris Dam (Figure 8.1) had been started at a point identified on the Corps of Engineers plans and using a dam design from the Bureau of Reclamation. Wheeler Dam followed quickly, and both were completed by 1936. By this time another three dams were under construction. The newly created Civilian Conservation Corps was put to work at once planting millions of tree seedlings on the steeper slopes of the basin to reduce soil erosion, and by the end of 1933 arrangements had been made with local agricultural colleges to run a major programme of farmer education. In 1934 the new phosphorus furnace at the Muscle Shoals former munitions (now chemical fertiliser) plant was installed and cheap fertiliser became available for use on the fields. These parts of the programme can be seen as an integrated attempt to plan for the improvement of the rural areas that the Tennessee Valley was at that stage.

However, much of what TVA attempted was controversial right from the beginning. This was partly due to the fact that it was imposed on the region by the US Congress, and that the local farmers were particularly conservative and defensive in their attitudes, especially when some of their best land was being drowned. Another factor which became important was that TVA had been established with a three-member board of directors appointed directly by the president. His initial choice had attempted to bring together three men with complementary experience to cover the wide-ranging aims of the programme, but they were

FIGURE 8.1 The basins of the Tennessee and Cumberland Rivers (after Bradshaw, 1984a), showing details of power-generating plants

unable to overcome the fundamental differences which existed between them. The chairman (A. Morgan) was an academic known for his interest in economic and social planning; the other two were a Tennessee agriculturalist (H. Morgan) and a lawyer who had specialised in cases involving the public generation of electricity (J. Lilienthal).

The chairman was responsible for some of the early attempts to incorporate broader local social and economic planning into the basic TVA objectives: a new town was built next to the Norris Dam, and its 'peoples' houses' were designed for those who would work in the factories which would use the electricity produced at the dam. But he found it difficult to relate to the attitudes of the local farmers, and they became antagonistic to him in public meetings. Some resented the Federal intrusion in any form, and preferred to die 'poor but proud'. Others appreciated assistance if it did not entail paternalistic or communal involvements. It soon became clear that the other two directors favoured a different strategy – that of producing and selling cheap power to stimulate economic development, rather than attempting to plan for every aspect of life in the Tennessee Valley. This latter approach was more popular among the farmers, since it left them more say in their own affairs.

A third set of antagonisms brought this internal debate to a head. Although the initial remit of TVA had only 'allowed' the sale of surplus electrical power, the local private power companies objected even to this modest clause as unfair competition. They had established a virtual monopoly of power production and prices were so high that smaller towns could not afford a supply of electricity. So TVA trod warily and the first contracts for the sale of its power were with such small towns as Tupelo, Mississippi, which had not been supplied by the private companies. However, the Rural Electrification Act of 1935 was important in encouraging the establishment of local co-operatives for distributing electrical power more widely, and the issue of private v. public power was brought to a head.

A series of court actions in the mid 1930s over the issue of these increasing sales of public electricity held back the greater utilisation of TVA power, but also focused attention on the possibility of TVA providing cheap power on a much larger scale than had been envisaged at first. The protests of the private power companies boomeranged by forcing TVA to establish its legal position; once established, new prospects were opened. This issue, combined with bad publicity over the differences between the directors of TVA, led to a congressional investigation of the agency in 1938. The result was that the original chairman was replaced by John Lilienthal, the public-power lawyer, and TVA was given the go-ahead to develop its sales of electricity.

8.4 TVS: THE YEARS OF 'POWER OBSESSION'

By 1940 TVA was poised to enter its major phase of growth and contribution to economic change within its basin. During this phase TVA concentrated on providing cheap electricity and improved navigation, rather than on the whole set of social and economic possibilities which had been opened up by the 1933 legislation. Half-a-dozen hydro-electric dams had been completed, and others were continued despite the diversion of resources to the war effort in 1941. Muscle Shoals was converted back to a munitions plant at first, then reconverted to manufacture fertilisers for the wartime efforts to produce more food. A new munitions plant was sited near Huntsville, Alabama, aluminium production was increased, and the initial centre for research on the atom bomb was established at Oak Ridge near Knoxville, Tennessee. All of these were the result of the local availability of cheap electricity, and led to the stimulation of demand for more and more power. The hydro-electric plants could not cope with this increased demand, and by the late 1940s there was a shift into the construction of coal-fired steam plants using coal from nearby Kentucky.

So began the period of demand-led economic development in the Tennessee basin (what has been termed the phase of 'power obsession'). By 1950, 80 per cent of the farms in the Valley had access to electricity (compared to 3 per cent in 1933 and 28 per cent in 1945). Over the next 20 years the average consumption of electricity per home in the Valley rose from 3000 kilowatt hours in 1950 to 14,000 kWh in 1970, while price rates dropped to half the US average by the early 1960s. The population of the Tennessee basin rose from 3 million in 1933 to over 7 million in 1980, and average family incomes were 80 per cent of the US norm by 1980. The combination of increasing population, affluence and power

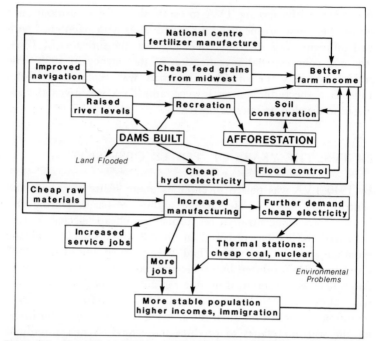

FIGURE 8.2 Changes in the Tennessee Valley: the linkages and multiplier effects resulting from TVA investments (after Bradshaw, 1984a). Not all the results were 'good', and few of them were planned to occur in the ways depicted

usage caused demand for electricity to grow by over six times between 1950 and 1980. This occurred despite the lack of new industry which used large quantities of electricity after the 1940s: new manufacturing plants came to the region, but mainly because of the low labour costs relative to other parts of the US.

The increasing demand for electricity was met by building more power plants. After 1959 TVA could borrow money publicly for this, and did not have to go to the US Congress for planning permission for every new plant. The promise of cheap power from nuclear plants caused TVA to become an innovator and initial entrant in this field, with its first plant being opened at Brown's Ferry in 1967. Even at the time of rising energy costs in 1973, TVA was planning to double its output of electricity within the next ten years by means of a programme to build large nuclear power stations. But by 1978 TVA itself was hit by rising costs imposed by higher fuel prices and the need to make modifications to its coal-fired plants to meet environmental legislation conditions. It was forced to raise its prices and to cancel some of the plans for further nuclear plants. In the mid 1980s further problems struck TVA as all its nuclear power plants were closed down due to faulty systems.

After 50 years of existence, TVA in the mid 1980s is still a formidable force, employing some 40,000 people and producing more electricity than any other utility in the US. It has had a major effect on its region – both in terms of altered landscape and in the economic well-being of the people (Figure 8.2). The switch of farming from row crops to a pastoral emphasis, and the planting of great numbers of trees turned the land from brown to green, and also reduced soil erosion and flooding. Urban-industrial growth was spawned by cheap electricity, both in the larger and also in many medium-sized towns. The new waterfront sites became popular for industry (with access to navigation), residences and recreational facilities.

8.5 TVA: AN EVALUATION

An evaluation of the role of TVA in conscious regional planning has to reach the conclusion that the agency, while fulfilling many of the individual items in its original remit, did not establish the direct control of social and economic development by integrated regional planning which its first chairman desired and which has become a sort of TVA mythology. This can be demonstrated in a number of ways.

Firstly, after the early Norris experience, TVA did not acquire more land by compulsory purchase order than it needed for each dam, the reservoir area and limited tributary areas on the surrounding slopes. Until the 1960s TVA left other aspects of local planning (e.g. even the rerouting of drowned roads) to the State of Tennessee, and had only very small amounts of money available to invest in what were essentially cosmetic changes (e.g. 'Operation Townlift' to help with the modernisation of downtown facilities in small towns).

Secondly, when TVA made attempts to get back into local planning in the 1960s, after the 'power obsession' years, it still failed to achieve anything. This was partly due to priorities within

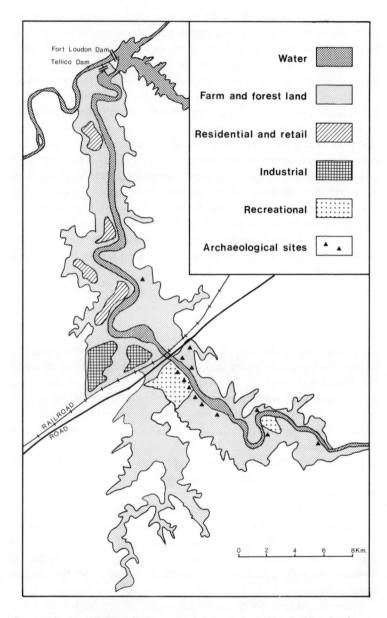

FIGURE 8.3 The Tellico Project: the land purchased and plans for its use
(from TVA report 1981)

TVA (where 90 per cent of employees were in the Power Division), but also due to inappropriate ideas, external events beyond TVA control ('bad luck'), and the fact that other approaches to local planning had by-passed what TVA was able to do. The building of the Melton Hill Dam in 1963 was the first in which TVA liaised closely with the State of Tennessee in all aspects of planning. This experience led to attempts to develop two further approaches to involvement in broader socio-economic planning by TVA.

The first attempt was the establishment of the Tributary Area Development programme in the 1960s, with the idea of providing a 'grassroots' means of evaluating local needs prior to encouraging economic development. This was a continuation of the earlier adherence to drainage basin units as the basis for local planning. The Tributary Areas were parts of the main drainage basin, divided along internal watersheds. The idea was put forward in 1961, but although 15 TADs had been designated by 1966, a combination of internal administrative difficulties and a lack of investment finance meant that the programme was regarded inside TVA as a failure by the 1980s. By this time other non-TVA agencies, based on groups of local government units, had been established by Federal and State authority to carry out the role expected of the TADs. This rendered the whole idea meaningless.

The second attempt was a major planned development linked to the Tellico Dam project begun in 1965 (Figure 8.3). This development involved the purchase of 22,000 acres in addition to the 16,000 required for the dam and reservoir. The extra land was to be used for a new town, Timberlake, which the Boeing Corporation contracted to build, and also for the siting of a variety of industrial and commercial enterprises taking advantage of the good road and rail links available. A thorough survey and land-suitability analysis was carried out for this area in the late 1960s, but delays were caused in the 1970s by the demand to produce an Environmental Impact Statement and then by objections based on the Endangered Species Act. These delays resulted in the withdrawal of the Boeing Corporation in 1975 due to the anticipated rising costs of its development, and since that time few firms have been attracted to the site. Although the dam was eventually completed and filled in 1979, TVA is now leasing the land it had expected to be instrumental in developing to local county authorities. They have now taken over the development process. This was the final blow to TVA interest in regional planning, and the agency now co-operates in only minor ways with other agencies.

8.6 TVA: CONCLUSIONS

The TVA experience has underlined a number of important points which affect consciously-directed regionalism within the United States. Firstly, it was a 'top-down' programme, initiated in Washington and directed from the Federal capital at least until the 1960s. It was not able to convince local people that it provided a partnership in planning, and the move to concentrate on generating electrical power was partly the result of this emphasis on national, rather than local, needs.

Secondly, the TVA programme focused on major public works, which have been the outcome of most federally-funded programmes. Going further than this smacks of interference in people's lives to most Americans, and such views were impressed on TVA officials by local people in the early days of the agency.

Thirdly, TVA never came to grips with the established political hierarchy of state and local government to the extent that it consulted them and worked co-operatively in planning. The governor of Tennessee spoke out against TVA at its inception, and much of what TVA did subsequently was without reference to local opinion. Although it had its headquarters at Knoxville, in the upper part of the Tennessee Valley, the agency retained an image of being subject to Washington and not responsive to the needs of the basin.

Fourthly, the TVA principle of regional planning within a drainage basin was never repeated elsewhere in the United States, although plans were drawn up in the 1940s for other river basin projects in the Upper Missouri and the Lower Columbia basins. However, some of the principles used in the TVA programme have been copied or developed in other parts of the world, as in the Volta River project of Ghana and the ill-fated Mekong River project of south-east Asia. The fact that TVA did not become a model for wider planning in the United States can be accounted for by the opposition it engendered in its early years, by the intervention of the Second World War and subsequent diversion of resources to achieve global political objectives, and by the fact that ideas on regional planning had changed by the time the next demand for federal action in this area came in the 1960s. Perhaps, above all, the use of a drainage basin – a 'geographical feature' – was shown to be inappropriate in a nation where most socio-economic planning is based on political units: counties, municipalities and states.

9. Public Policy and Regionalism: II. The Appalachian Regional Commission and other Federal Approaches to Regional Planning in the 1960s

9.1 INTRODUCTION

In the 1960s there were a number of attempts in the United States to plan within a regional base, although none attracted funding on the scale of the nationwide agencies (Figure 9.1). The term, 'regional commission' was used in a rather confusing way for several quite distinct approaches. The Appalachian Regional Commission was designated to apply to all, or part, of thirteen states, and was given a variety of powers and links to other programmes. It was also independent of other Federal agencies, and was supplied with at least reasonable amounts of money to carry out its work, and so was able to develop into a mature agency.

The Economic Development Administration and the 'Title V' Regional Commissions were created so that groups of states could work together for the purposes of economic development, but never had the advantages of the range of programmes, independence or finances available to ARC. Although the concept involved was similar to that of ARC in some ways, these other regional

138

Dept./Agency	General Development		Economic Development	
	Amount	Percentage	Amount	Percentage
Commerce(EDA)			400	9.0 *
ARC			300	6.7 *
Title V Reg. Commns.			64	2.2 *
TVA	45	0.2		*
HUD	3,600	12.0	550	12.3
USDA	5,780	19.4	927	20.8
EPA	4,500	15.1		
DOL			1,880	42.2
HEW	650	2.2		
DOT	10,500	35.2		
SBA	3,100	10.4	100	2.2
Other	1,647	5.5	203	4.6
	29,822	100.0	4,424	100.0

FIGURE 9.1   Federal funds voted for various types of development assistance during Federal Year 1978. Those with a regional emphasis are marked with an asterisk (from House, 1983)

commissions did not achieve any great success and were discontinued in 1981.

In 1968 a series of four Federal Regional Councils was established, and later extended to ten covering the nation. The idea of these Councils was to co-ordinate the work of Federal agencies, but this occurred slowly, and there was never any attempt to link these with the Regional Commissions.

The idea of river basin units was reintroduced in the Water Resources Act of 1965, but in a different manner from TVA, and without the powers or funding. Finally, the term 'regional commission' is also applied to smaller areas encompassing the metropolitan areas of many large cities, where there have been efforts to co-ordinate the planning of some functions. Such metropolitan co-ordinating units are more commonly termed 'Councils of Government' (COGs), and have a different basis from the larger regional commissions extending across several states.

Their work is assessed in Chapter 10. The discussion in this chapter focuses on the Appalachian Regional Commission, and on the Title V Regional Commissions.

9.2 THE ORIGINS AND PRECURSORS OF ARC

For thirty years TVA remained as the sole example of Federal intervention in regional planning – an example which had been rejected as any basis for wider application within the nation. Although plans had been made to extend similar planning to such areas as the Upper Missouri (1944) and the Lower Columbia river basins, nothing materialised after the Second World War and political support for such agencies was reduced.

By the late 1950s concern was being expressed over the backward economic conditions prevalent in the Appalachian region, and also in some other largely rural parts of the US. The Appalachian situation came to the national notice in a dramatic way during the presidential campaign of John Kennedy in 1960, and so gained prominence among the causes demanding political attention. Faced with major challenges in the Democratic Primary race, and then against Richard Nixon, the Kennedy campaign focused on the need to overcome glaring inequalities of opportunity within the nation at a time when most Americans (like the British at the time) 'had never had it so good'. This was not an easy message to get across, but the major use of television in this campaign ensured that the shoeless children and tar-paper shacks of West Virginia would shame Americans into a more liberal stance towards the needs of such poor people.

Kennedy won the election (just), but his early years of office did not achieve much in the way of legislation to deal with the problems his campaign had highlighted. Although advocated by some of the 'prophets' within Appalachia (Caudill, 1962), the TVA-type of regional solution could not be repeated, and the US Congress was not keen on passing programmes which brought benefits to a limited part of the nation.

The Area Redevelopment Act, passed soon after Kennedy took over power in 1961, provided limited amounts of money in grant-aid packages which could be claimed by a third of the counties in the US. To qualify for such assistance the county had to produce an Overall Economic Development Plan and provide 50 per cent matching funds. Urban places were better fitted for this than rural because they had established planning teams and could provide the matching funds for each project. None of the essentially rural counties in Appalachia obtained very much money from this process. Even the improvements added to this legislation in 1962 made little difference. However, although this programme did not meet the needs of Appalachia, or of other lagging regions in the US, it provided some valuable insights to what could be possible and also gave experience to personnel who administered later programmes.

Eight of the governors of states with part of their territory in Appalachia had lobbied the presidential candidates in 1960. Further flood devastation in 1962–3 brought them together again, and in April 1963 President Kennedy set up the President's Appalachian Regional Commission (PARC) to prepare a report and legislation for the needs of the region. Kennedy was assassinated later in that year, and the first attempt at Appalachian legislation was not passed as submitted in 1964. But, following the sweeping victory by Lyndon Johnson at the end of 1964, the Appalachian Regional Development Act was passed in March 1965. The fact that it was passed was due, not merely to the spirit of the assassinated President Kennedy, or to the political power of President Johnson, but also to the presence of so many politicians with Appalachian backgrounds in prominent committee positions in the US Congress. Like TVA, it was one of the first products of a rare phase in which many liberal laws were passed, but had a very different basis.

The PARC report of 1964 highlighted economic, environmental, social and political problems within Appalachia. The economic conditions in the early 1960s were the particular concern of the business community. Low incomes, high unemployment, overdependence on a single industry, and lack of modern infrastructure were common features of local reports produced at this time in such widely separated districts as eastern Kentucky, northern Georgia and western Pennsylvania. The northern part of Appalachia was still a major base of the steel industry, but the dependence on such heavy industry was beginning to have adverse effects in that area. The central part of Appalachia was in deep depression due to low prices and poor markets for its coal. The southern subregion was beginning to experience economic growth, but still had poor facilities to support this. Throughout Appalachia the local economies appeared to possess little ability to modernise: it was concluded by many local businessmen and politicians that outside assistance was needed.

The environmental problems of Appalachia had resulted from the unfettered exploitation of timber, coal and other mineral resources. There had been a progressive expansion of this exploitation from northern Appalachia to central and southern areas between the mid nineteenth century and the early twentieth century. This had produced unattractive landscapes, polluted streams and reduced economic prospects. Flooding became more frequent and devastating as a result, and this produced common ground for the governors of Appalachian states. When they came together to ask the Federal government for assistance in replacing the great number of bridges washed away in the 1963 floods, they also recognised the need for a broader set of programmes which might be applied to Appalachia.

Social deprivation was a further source of concern: the isolated peoples of Appalachia were regarded outside as backward 'hill-billies'. This resulted from a combination of entrenched social traditions, low levels of education in all-age village schools, poor health care (reflected in high infant-mortality rates) and difficult access to larger centres of population and employment. As the more enterprising young families moved out in large numbers during the 1950s, the remaining population was ageing, had little potential or wish to modernise, and so the old order was retained. Even when families moved out of their home region to find employment in the northern industrial cities, they often ended up in 'poor-white ghettos' in Cincinnati, Chicago or Cleveland, having few skills and so unable to compete for the best-paying jobs.

The political environment throughout much of central and southern Appalachia remained almost feudal, dominated by a few families or the coal company managers. Local politics was single-party, and many jobs were handed out in relation to political allegiance. The inward-looking nature of local politics was also enhanced by the small size of political units: many of the counties in central Appalachia have fewer than 10,000 people living in them. This added to the conservative stance of society within Appalachia and thus to the difficulty of making changes. Reforms could not be initiated locally or introduced from outside, and those who felt helpless to do anything about their plight became alienated from society. The political and social state of Appalachia was subject to comments by academics and political activists, and placed in a prominent place in the overall list of problems affecting the region.

However, the Appalachian Regional Development Act of 1965 appeared to many observers at the time, and into the 1970s, to have been shorn of any real ability to make changes in these conditions (Figure 9.2). The emphasis placed by the PARC Report on environmental programmes within the mountainous region was dropped in deference to objections from states which felt that such investment in Appalachia would threaten their own farming communities; a suggestion to make a study of Appalachian water resource development was not taken further; and the utilisation of timber resources was hedged around with administrative deterrents. At the same time, the need to develop the human resources of the region was separated from this particular Act, since President Johnson had determined to submit a wider-ranging set of proposals for the whole nation. Thus, the 1965 Appalachian Act appeared to concentrate on a major road-building programme, with subsidiary programmes to encourage vocational education and to establish some demonstration programmes in health-care delivery. The headquarters for the Appalachian Regional Commission were set up in Washington, and this was also criticised as divorcing the agency from its region.

Even these programmes were difficult to operate in the first few years, since each aspect had to be funded through the major established Federal government agencies, and this slowed the impact of ARC on its region. Despite such an inauspicious beginning, and considerable early criticism concerning its lack of powers and its heavy reliance on the road-building programme, ARC gradually exerted an increasing influence within its region. By 1979 it was being suggested to the US Congress that its structure should act as the model on which future regional economic development within the US should be based. The 1979 Bill to extend the Appalachian legislation for a further five years was combined with the extension of the Public Works and Economic Development Act, and had that ambitious principle built into it. But it was not passed before the Carter administration handed over power to the Reagan administration in 1980, and the latter had no interest in supporting regional development programmes.

APPALACHIA: CHANGING PERCEPTIONS OF PLANNING NEEDS AND MODIFICATIONS MADE IN THE LEGISLATION

PROGRAMME	PARC, 1964	APPALACHIAN REGIONAL DEV ACT 1965	CHANGES SINCE 1965
HIGHWAYS	First priority: Interstate Highway system bypasses much, especially in Central subregion. Recommended system of 2150 miles, plus 500 miles access roads ($1.2 billion).	*Section 201* Appalachian Development Highway System: 2350 miles, plus 1000 miles access roads ($840 million).	Increases in both funds and road lengths, 1967–79. Standards set for lower costs; system agreed by states and built by them in short sections; major impact on commuting.
NATURAL RESOURCES AND ENVIRONMENT	A major emphasis: *Water resources.* Construction by TVA, COE, FHA ($36 millions). Local water, sewage systems ($10m) *Agriculture.* Programme to cut cropland and expand pasture ($22 millions). *Timber.* $7 millions for research into hardwood use and processing.	Few recommendations incorporated, but some via existing programmes ($43 million); a number of compromises. *Section 206* study by COE ($5m), but few projects resulted. *Section 214* Supplemental Funds used. *Section 203* Land Stabilisation, but few funds made available. Pasture improvement dropped; lack of funds. *Section 204* set up Timber Development Organisations, but restrictions made them unworkable.	Major shift from resource development to environmental concern over resource exploitation. Natural resources seen as playing a small part in development (extractive industry <5% employment, and declining). Narrow programmes at start changed to the creation of new land for economic development, then to comprehensive pollution control.

	Minerals. $3 millions to expand coal markets, reduce environmental impacts. *Power.* Study of region's contribution to USA production. *Recreation.* Endorsed pending proposals.	*Section 205* Mine Restoration (of major interest to Pennsylvania). Clause forbids ARC funds to be used to produce/distribute electricity/gas. (No reference).	ARC funded major studies.
EDUCATION	Heavy emphasis on vocational education. Other aspects left to proposed poverty agency; no HE or school proposals.	*Section 211* Vocational Education funds. *Section 214* Supplemental Funds could be used.	Broader role evolved with regional coordination of facilities (RESAs), leading into HE; Early Childhood; professional and technical training.
HEALTH	Recommended demonstration regional health centres ($40 millions).	*Section 202* provided $41 millions for construction; $28 millions for operation – a revolutionary step.	Construction gave way to operation emphasis; local councils; manpower training; clinics; primary care focus.
HOUSING	Major problem identified: repairs, dilapidation; inadequate plumbing.	(No specific recommendations).	Soon had requests for advice; policy led to *Section 207*, 1967; later expanded further and use of HUD.
SUPPLEMENTAL FUNDS		*Section 214*, to 'top up' other federal funds where local tax base low. Broad range of programmes possible.	States determine usage – mainly in voc. education, health, airports, water and sewer: 80% human resources.

FIGURE 9.2 The changes in the Appalachian programme resulting from the 'public policy process' (from Bradshaw, 1984a). The proposals made by the President's Appalachian Regional Commission (PARC, 1964) were modified greatly in the Appalachian Regional Development Act of 1965), and further changes have occurred in the 20 years since

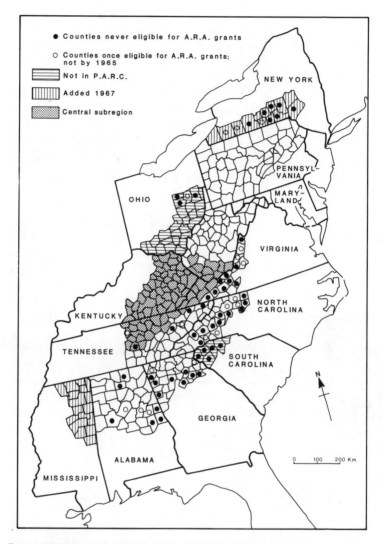

FIGURE 9.3   The evolution of the Appalachian Regional Commission 'region'
(after Bradshaw, 1985):
(A) Eight states contributed to PARC in 1964.
(B) Ohio and South Carolina were added for the 1965 legislation.
(C) New York and Mississippi were added in 1967.
There was controversy during the passing of the legislation over the inclusion
of many counties which did not have great economic problems

9.3 REASONS BEHIND THE SUCCESS OF ARC

A number of factors was responsible for the changes in perception of this programme from one which was weak and unrelated to the real needs of the region to one which was widely regarded – especially within the region – as successful.

Firstly, the congressional support for ARC was strengthened. The first Appalachian Governors' meeting represented eight states; by the 1965 legislation parts of Ohio and South Carolina had been added, and in 1967 parts of New York and even Mississippi were tacked on to the ARC region (Figure 9.3). This meant that 26 senators in Washington had an interest in keeping the ARC programme alive. However, it is also significant that the main continuing support for ARC came from the House of Representatives, with its greater emphasis on the internal and local concerns of the United States. Overwhelming votes for the continuation of ARC were repeated in the House into the 1980s despite the Reagan administration opposition to such programmes. This support was based on local convictions that ARC was doing a useful job, and also on the ability of the Washington ARC office staff to maintain frequent contact with its legislative support.

Secondly, the programmes administered through ARC soon became consolidated into 'highway' and 'non-highway', and this gave greater flexibility for their application. The early arrangement of working through the major Federal agencies was discontinued after 1967, and so ARC gained independence and confidence. Then, the much-touted human resources programmes of the Johnson era were not as effective as had been hoped, and many declined or were closed in the early 1970s. The effect of this was that many of the issues these other programmes had tried to address came within the ARC province, and could be co-ordinated within local areas.

Thirdly, a number of aspects of the Appalachian legislation, which were initially seen as untried and unlikely to succeed, eventually came to be regarded as the major contributions of the programme. The idea for the establishment of local development districts (LDDs), formed of groups of counties within the thirteen states, was based on the experience of one or two localities within Appalachia, particularly in northern Georgia and eastern Kentucky. The LDDs thus arose from locally perceived expressions of the need to co-ordinate planning and avoid overlap, waste and the missing-out of some areas. They were mentioned rather tentatively in the 1965 legislation, and were slow to develop in some states: West Virginia did not have them functioning fully until 1973. By the mid 1970s the LDDs had become the main 'working parts' of the ARC process. They linked local planning needs with State co-ordination and the Federal grant-aid sources. They became designated as the agencies responsible for the local overview of all Federal grant-aid spending, and so gained an important and central place in local access to Federal grant-aid funds. A major contribution they were able to make was to facilitate the distribution of grant-aid to rural as well as urban places. It is not without significance that the development of LDDs in Appalachia in the 1970s coincided with a return of many people to rural areas and with rising socio-economic well-being throughout Appalachia. It would be going too far to suggest that the LDD process was directly responsible for these trends, but most local people would assert that they helped to make it possible.

Fourthly, another major factor in the ultimate success of ARC was the fact that it could augment the normal Federal 50 per cent grant-aid for a project to 80 per cent (and to 100 per cent for some health-care projects) with Supplemental Funds. This also had the effect of allowing rural places to benefit from the availability of Federal grant-aid. In combination with the supply of funds by ARC to pay LDD staff, the Supplemental Funds became important in delivering grant-aid funding to many parts of Appalachia which had previously not been able to get as far as asking for assistance. The LDD staff put together funding packages which utilised the grant-aid programmes of agencies such as Housing & Urban Development (HUD) with loans from other agencies such as Farmers' Home Administration (FHA) and added a proportion of Supplemental Funds.

The impact of these processes grew during the 1970s, as LDDs were established through Appalachia: the 397 counties within the ARC 'region' were organised in 69 LDDs. Each LDD was governed by a majority of local elected officials from counties and municipalities, together with representatives of business and other sectors of the communities. This resulted in co-operation and bargaining over the distribution of grant-aid projects and led to each county and municipality receiving some assistance over time.

Thus rural counties which had been inhibited in the process of economic development, and in the local provision of health and education services, were able to develop and attract employment opportunities. This also had the effect of overturning the concept of 'growth centre' investment which had also been built into the legislation as the fashionable planning idea of the 1960s. Previous experience of spreading grant-aid thinly over the entire US had caused the 1965 legislators to view the growth centre idea favourably, since it provided a mechanism whereby limited funds could be concentrated in a few places and be seen to have an impact. However, the growth centre concept is one which has to be imposed on an area from outside – the hallmark of 'top–down' planning – whereas the LDDs made it possible to develop 'bottom–up' planning based on locally expressed needs co-ordinated at the state level.

9.4 SOME IMPACTS OF ARC

A number of examples of the local and wider impacts of these programmes can be cited to demonstrate how the ARC process has worked. Its impact in terms of favour with state and national politicians can be gauged from the fact that it had received continued support in the House of Representatives in particular, and also in the Senate until 1980. Then, when President Reagan threatened to close down ARC in 1981, the state governors lobbied for its continuation on the basis that the process would be continued in any case. They persuaded Congress to pass a 'Finish-up' programme with more restricted (two-thirds of late 1970s) funding to last until 1987, and then Congress voted funds each year against the president's advice. The House of Representatives even passed motions to extend the authorisation into the 1990s.

The road programme, so heavily criticised in the early years, was shown to have been particularly important in the late 1970s redevelopment of the Appalachian coal industry in competition with new coal-mining areas farther west (Figure 9.4). Sufficient evidence was also to hand to demonstrate that the new manufacturing industries, which had moved into Appalachia and provided such an upturn in the region's economy in the 1970s, were sited as near as possible to the new roads and had taken

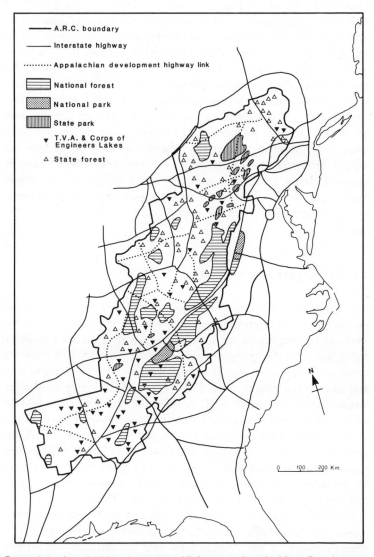

FIGURE 9.4 Appalachia: Interstate Highways, Appalachian Development Highways, Forests, Parks and Lakes (after Bradshaw, 1985). This map provides an indication of the impact of Federal programmes in the region

advantage of the ARC funds to build access roads to industrial parks.

Studies of a number of LDDs have also shown how ARC and its co-ordination of associated programmes has been able to bring about improvements in local planning. In Huntsville, Alabama, which became the centre of the NASA rocket-making industry in the 1960s, the side-effects of industrial and population expansion at that time provided a nightmare for local authorities before the days of the LDDs. The shortages of housing and good schooling, as well as water and sewage services, meant that heavy additional Federal funding was necessary at short notice to support this unanticipated growth. However, when NASA began running down its operations in the late 1960s and early 1970s, the LDD organisation was able to co-ordinate the change and to attract 15,000 new jobs to replace those lost by the NASA decline.

In rural areas of central Tennessee, eastern Kentucky and West Virginia, the first proper water supply, educational and health services have been provided. Eastern Kentucky was a by-word for depressed economic conditions in the mid 1960s, and up to 75 per cent of the population aged 15–34 had left since 1950 due to a lack of jobs in the coal industry and an absence of alternatives. The revival of the coal industry in these low-sulphur coalfields in the mid 1970s was dramatic, and brought back most of those who had migrated to other parts of the nation, but it was made possible by the combination of improving markets for coal with the presence of new roads, schools, hospitals, shopping centres and also by new attitudes to co-operation between local governments.

One of the most convincing cases of LDD operation is in eastern Tennessee, in the centre of TVA territory. Here the provision of better transport links and industrial park facilities throughout the LDD territory has finally enabled the district to make the most of the potential provided by TVA. Some formerly depressed, ex-coal-mining counties, and other rural counties, now have access to a variety of employment opportunities. Development around the expanding city of Knoxville has been spread out, rather than concentrated in a small area, due to the widespread availability of good roads, water and sewage facilities and jobs. Such a spread of economic well-being would not have occurred if the growth centre policy had been continued.

9.5 ARC AND PLANNING IN THE UNITED STATES

The Appalachian Regional Commission has never had an overall plan for the economic development of its region. It has been criticised for this on a number of occasions, including during the 1975 revision of legislation in the US Congress. However, it is difficult to see how ARC could have developed a plan for its whole region, given the constitutional role played by each state. Each state has a distinctive political stance, which may change every few years with the election of a new governor. Any central plan would have been limited to general platitudes.

The closest approximations to such a plan have been formulated by the LDDs since 1975 in their Areawide Action Plans. These are based on surveys of local conditions, strengths and needs, leading to the identification of a set of priorities for funding projects within the LDD. Perhaps the LDD is the most appropriate geographical unit for such planning if sufficient detail is to be included. The growth of confidence in the LDD agencies has led to wider consultation through public meetings. The LDD centred on Asheville, North Carolina, holds what it calls its 'Mountain Marathon': an annual tour of the outlying parts of the district to hold discussions with local inhabitants over the previous projects and the proposals for the coming year. Other LDDs have been following this example.

ARC has thus provided more of a process than a plan – a process to deliver grant-aid to rural localities in particular, and one which links the main levels of local, state and federal government through both 'bottom–up' and 'top–down' attempts to develop local resources, human and physical.

Although the emphasis in this chapter has been placed on the development of political structures to facilitate the delivery of Federal grant-aid to disadvantaged areas such as rural Appalachia in the 1960s and 1970s, little would have been achieved without the interventions of a host of individuals who have been instrumental in devising, developing and operating the legislation at Federal, state and local levels. The history of ARC since its inception has been a catalogue of coincidences and of the personal promotion of particular ideas. One of the most influential people behind the programme was John Whisman, who began as a businessman in eastern Kentucky in the 1950s. When he took over the chairmanship of the Junior Chambers of Commerce in the state he attempted to establish economic development in the depressed eastern counties. This led him to work with the governor of Kentucky, who was one of the leaders pressuring President Kennedy for action in Appalachia in the early 1960s. Whisman became the executive secretary of PARC and eventually the state governors' representative at ARC headquarters in Washington. Much of the progress of the legislation was due to Whisman's influence and readiness with forms of words to fit the development programme.

But Whisman was not the only individual to influence the nature and progress of ARC. The programme was passed by the US Congress because so many of the vital committees were chaired by senators and congressmen with Appalachian origins or sympathies. In particular, Senator Jennings Randolph of West Virginia had a major role in promoting and maintaining support for ARC.

The extent to which the thirteen states benefited from the ARC programmes has depended on the people in the governors' offices in the state capitals and the ways in which they have encouraged LDDs to develop. And the LDDs have succeeded in recruiting a range of quality staff who have managed to work with able local politicians.

These points concerning the importance of individuals in the design and operation of a particular example of public policy are made to emphasise the manner in which such policies originate and are operated. There is no process by which a group of experts assess the issues involved and write a piece of legislation which is automatically passed by the US Congress. Individuals are involved at every stage, and their experience, interests and powers of persuasion are reflected in whether the legislation gets to the floor of Congress, whether it is passed as an Act and then whether it is administered successfully. At each stage there is a combination of debate, trade-off and compromise. The social economic and political structures of the time affect whether the issue will get on the agenda for public policy in the first place, and individuals and groups then determine how the eventual legislation will modify the society in which they live.

9.6 EDA AND THE 'TITLE V' REGIONAL COMMISSIONS

Later in 1965, the Public Works and Economic Development Act established the Economic Development Administration and the prospect of a set of regional commissions to cover the rest of the US under Title V of the Act. The EDA has been regarded by some as a rival to ARC, but EDA had a remit which potentially covered the whole US. The greatest similarity to ARC was in its Economic Development Districts, which resembled LDDs in being formed of groups of counties within states. They had different rules for the composition of their Boards than the LDDs (being somewhat more 'democratic'), and had more rigid criteria for the recognition of growth centres. Within the Appalachian region the EDD and LDD agencies reached an accommodation, and were combined under the same roof by the mid 1970s, but outside this region the EDDs did not have so much impact. With the reduction in funding for EDA in the 1970s, cuts were made in the supply of administrative costs to the EDDs.

One of the main difficulties faced by EDA was its position as a minor agency within the Department of Commerce. It was thus bound by the working rules of its Department, and not as free as ARC to innovate. Within Appalachia it was seen by the LDD officials as more prone to red tape. It was also more difficult for it to muster political support at times of crisis and, whereas its funding had been more than twice that of ARC in the mid 1970s, it was reduced to a similar level in the 1980s. EDA shifted its position on its objectives during the course of the twenty years from 1965. It began by focusing on the 'worst first' areas of lagging non-metropolitan hinterlands, but soon found that these areas were intractable and moved to supporting areas with potential for growth. During the 1970s its growth centre policy was so dispersed that almost every small town became a growth centre and eventually the idea was abandoned since there were not the funds to achieve such a widespread application. Then there was another move to attend to the plight of the inner city poor.

The Title V Regional Commissions were also tied to the Department of Commerce, and suffered accordingly (Estall, 1982). Only five other commissions were set up by 1967, but new ones were added up to 1979 (Figure 9.5). However, these commissions

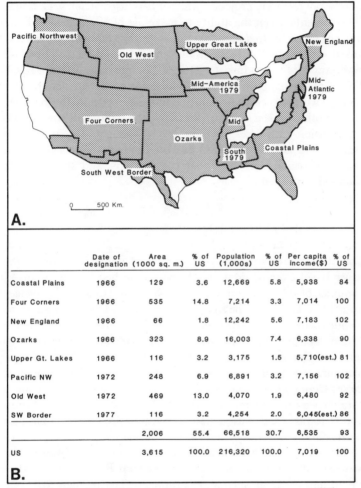

	Date of designation	Area (1000 sq. m.)	% of US	Population (1,000s)	% of US	Per capita income($)	% of US
Coastal Plains	1966	129	3.6	12,669	5.8	5,938	84
Four Corners	1966	535	14.8	7,214	3.3	7,014	100
New England	1966	66	1.8	12,242	5.6	7,183	102
Ozarks	1966	323	8.9	16,003	7.4	6,338	90
Upper Gt. Lakes	1966	116	3.2	3,175	1.5	5,710(est.)	81
Pacific NW	1972	248	6.9	6,891	3.2	7,156	102
Old West	1972	469	13.0	4,070	1.9	6,480	92
SW Border	1977	116	3.2	4,254	2.0	6,045(est.)	86
		2,006	55.4	66,518	30.7	6,535	93
US		3,615	100.0	216,320	100.0	7,019	100

B.

FIGURE 9.5 The 'Title V' Regional Commissions (from House, 1983)
(A) Their extent in 1981, just before being closed down.
(B) Details of the Regional Commissions existing in 1977

bore only a faint resemblance to ARC, and their existence was ended without any great objections when President Reagan came to power in 1981. The main reason for the lack of impact by these Title V commissions was the low level of funding allotted to them in total – of the annual order of a twentieth of that to ARC alone. This meant that some of the Title V commissions spent this money merely on research projects, while others used it for very limited developments. Even the ability to make use of Supplemental Funds was not taken up to a great extent, since the commissions were not linked closely to the local equivalents of the LDDs. There was never any attempt to link the Title V Commissions with the EDDs. The Appalachian Regional Commission was an independent agency, with one co-chairman appointed directly by the president and another taken up in turn by the state governors. The combination of higher funding levels and the structure of its organisation meant that ARC has been much more effective in its operating region than the other commissions, and should not be confused with them.

9.7 OTHER APPROACHES

The 1965 Water Resources Act proposed under its Title II that River Basin Commissions should be established for the basinwide planning of water resources. They were thus different in concept from TVA. However, the southern and south-western states rejected the idea, and even those areas which did establish the Commissions seldom got further than investigating immediate problems and certainly did not achieve comprehensive, joint and co-ordinated planning. As in the case of the Title V Regional Commissions, these Commissions lacked powers to act and also finances. Established by a different process, the Interstate Compacts affecting the Delaware and Susquehanna river basins were much more successful.

Another essentially regional approach by the Federal government was the establishment from 1968 of Federal Regional Councils to co-ordinate Federal agency programmes. Ten of these cover the nation, but they have not been totally successful in getting agreement between agencies on their administrative regional boundaries, and there was no link to the Title V Commissions at all. These Councils act purely for the benefit of Federal agency co-operation and have no links with the State governments.

In addition to these major regional approaches at the Federal level, there have been a number of attempts at the more local level, mainly in the context of organising the delivery of particular services. Most of these attempts are related to the mid-twentieth-century emergence of metropolitan regions, and the need to co-ordinate some aspects across the region made up often of over a hundred separate local jurisdictions. The 'regions' involved in these schemes are not so large as those discussed earlier in this chapter, but usually include several counties. They are thus closest in size to the LDDs. They are often referred to as Regional Councils of Government (or COGs), and are discussed more fully in the next chapter.

9.8 SUBSTATE REGIONALISM

It is instructive to put these various Federal attempts at regional planning in the context of the pattern of local government in the United States. Many of the local government divisions were instituted in a time when there was less mobility and the population was dispersed and rural. There are approximately 75,000 distinct local governments in the US: 3044 counties, 18,517 municipalities, 17,000 townships, 15,780 independent school districts and 23,885 other special districts. This confusing mass of entities is commonly being combined out of need in a number of multipurpose 'areawide' bodies such as the LDDs and COGs, but even in this there is no set pattern.

It is important to realise this situation, and the fact that Federal policies are mainly articulated through programmes which can deliver grant-aid to localities through the medium of areawide planning agencies such as the LDDs. This is most successful in the rural areas today, and the metropolitan areas with continuing fragmentation of local government provide a more difficult situation. This is the subject of the next chapter.

9.9 CONCLUSIONS

The study of the varied Federal attempts at regional planning within the US, and the listing of the number of substate units of local government, has demonstrated the difficulties faced by legislative approaches in that nation. The state-based division of the US, the negative attitudes to Federal 'interference' at state and local levels, and the devotion to public works grant-aid rather than welfare programmes, all impose their particular patterns. Within this context, the TVA programme achieved much in terms of stimulating economic growth through providing cheap electricity, but not what was expected by some of its original visionaries in terms of rural-based integrated planning or social engineering. The Title V Commissions were smothered at birth by the combination of insufficient funds and the link to a small agency in the Department of Commerce. The Appalachian Regional Commission has been more effective due to its independence among Federal agencies, and its ability to satisfy locally articulated needs. It thus stands out as the most important of the various attempts to enshrine regionalism in legislation by the US Congress.

Within the US there is a major debate between those who believe that there is no need for any sort of formal regional pattern of planning for economic development, and those who feel that such a formal basis would enable particular regions to make the most of their strengths as well as to patch up the weaknesses. The latter view takes forward the approaches of the 1950s and 1960s, which were based on assistance to poor regions in order to bring them up towards the national levels of economic and social well-being. It was expressed in the 1979 debate in Congress over the future of the Appalachian Regional Commission and the Title V Commissions (US Congress, 1979), when there was considerable sympathy for a revised regional division of the US to form the basis for LDD-type planning across the nation. However, the arguments over this continued, without resolution, until President Reagan was elected, and there has been no central sympathy for any measure of this type by his administration. It is still possible that such a debate will resurface when a new administration comes to power. So many of the issues in society demand a local, or regional, rather than a centralised, national, solution. For government planning to be effective it needs to maintain contact with local circumstances and perceptions of need.

10. Public Policy and Regionalism: III. Urban Issues

10.1 INTRODUCTION

The major inequalities in the United States have shifted from rural to inner-urban locations since the 1950s. Although the problem areas involved take up less space, the populations are just as great, and many of the issues have a geographical dimension. Metropolitan areas in the United States with 2 million people or more occupy the same space as Greater London in the UK with its 8 million residents. In addition, the links of these large metropolitan areas with the surrounding places give them a major influence on the economy, society and politics of those places. Issues which affect major metropolitan areas in the US are thus of regional significance.

This chapter will assess the nature of interactions between public policies and the changes in the built environments of major metropolitan areas within the US. There has never been a specific urban policy in the sense that the TVA and ARC programmes in particular applied to the problems of specific regions. What has emerged in the middle and later part of the twentieth century is a mixture of policies designed to have an impact on some of the problems evident in inner-city areas, and a number of other policies which have had an indirect impact on the ways in which metropolitan areas have grown. The result has often been confused and even contradictory, and has to be viewed in the context of the general reluctance of United States Federal governments to interefere in the essentially economic processes at work.

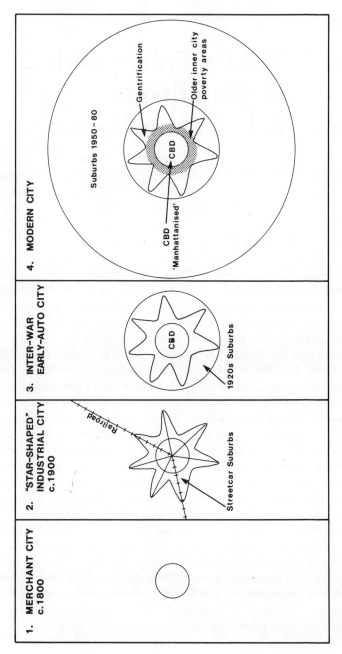

10.2 OVERCROWDED CITIES OF THE 1940s

By the end of the Second World War large American cities had become overcrowded due to a slow-down in building during the previous 20 years. A major phase in the growth of cities took place from 1860–1915 due to the expansion of manufacturing plants and the influx of workers from rural areas and from abroad. By the beginning of the First World War 'star-shaped' cities had grown due to the extension of industry along railroad lines and of housing along the electric street-car lines. Another phase of residential expansion occurred in the prosperous 1920s, when the early impact of automobile and truck led to the infilling of the spaces between the points of the star by dormitory suburbs with access to railroad commuting (Figure 10.1). These developments took place in an economic environment which allowed little Federal political intervention.

This phase of city expansion slowed down with the economic depression of the 1930s, when there was little private or local public money to invest in new buildings, and the Second World War then diverted available finance into the war effort. During the 1920s nearly 10 million housing units were added, but from 1930 to 1945 only just over 7 million (i.e. the rate of building was halved). However, the population continued to grow in size (1930 US total 123 million; 1945 141 million) and many manufacturing plants had moved to the outskirts of cities where there was land for the expanding factories.

Little was done in this phase by the Federal government to alleviate the increasing densities of urban population, but some crucial links were forged. The largest cities reacted against the difficulties of getting measures through their state legislatures, which were still dominated by rural interests. The big-city political leaders supported President Roosevelt in his bid for power, and then had direct access to Federal agencies in Washington – enabling them to go over the heads of state officials. In the New Deal years of the 1930s the Federal government, through the 1934 National Housing Act, established low-interest mortgages, backed up with insurance by the government, to encourage more people to own

FIGURE 10.1 Stages in the morphological evolution of US cities

their residences, but this had only a small impact before and during the war.

10.3 RAPID GROWTH AND DIFFERENTIATION OF CITIES, 1959–70

At the end of the Second World War American cities expanded rapidly: 16 million housing units were added in the US between 1945–60, and a further 10 million in the 1960s. An increasingly large proportion of these units were owner-occupier single-family houses, and this type of growth in the built environment around cities resulted in the development of suburban sprawl. This period also saw a rapid growth in the total United States population, with high rates of natural increase during the 'baby boom' combined with renewed immigration. The total population rose from 141 million in 1945 to 181 million in 1960 (double the 1930–45 rate) and 205 million in 1970.

As those who could afford the new housing moved out of the older parts of the cities, they left behind the poorer groups. There was also a major movement of people from rural areas and small towns into the larger metropolitan centres at this time, and these people went to inner-city low-cost housing or to the new suburbs if they could afford it. Much of the older housing was occupied by the black people who moved into cities from the southern rural areas, and this added to the movement of white middle-class families to the suburbs. This latter process has been termed 'white flight', but such 'push' factors were probably of minor importance compared to the 'pull' of the new housing and more attractive locations. The result is not debated: the largest cities became divided between the richer outer suburbs ('City of Superfluity' of Bunge's Detroit, 1975) and the poorer inner cities ('City of Death').

Much has been written about the impact of Federal government policies during this period (Davies, 1983, provides a good summary). The initial policies built on the 1934 National Housing Act encouraging families to own their homes. The 1944 Serviceman's Readjustment Act also provided low-interest mortgages and guaranteed them for those leaving military service at the end of the war. Then there were income tax deductions for those buying their own homes. Owner-occupation rose from 48 per cent in 1945 to 63 per cent of all housing units in 1970. Although these policies were aimed at the whole nation, they had a geographically specific impact in the suburbs of major metropolitan areas.

The relocation of middle-income and upper-income families was further enhanced by Federal grants for additional road-building, first for what are known as Federal Primary routes and, after 1956, for the Inter-state Highway System which built the largest system of limited-access highways in the world. These improved roads played an important part in focusing economic development on the largest cities and in differentiating between the inner and outer city. They allowed the trucking industry to compete with the railroads for freight transport, and this led to the relocation of industry on the outskirts of cities. In addition, these roads enabled commuters to live further away from their places of work and thus also encouraged the building of new outer suburbs around the major metropolitan centres. The built-over area of many major cities doubled between 1945 and 1970.

Both the financial inducements to home-ownership and the road-building programme resulted in deprivation for those in the inner cities between 1950 and 1970. The growth of the outer suburbs meant that there was less money available for those wishing to buy housing in the inner city. Banks and other loan institutions, together with the Federal mortgage insurance, tended to restrict loans to 'economically sound' areas. This often meant excluding areas of declining economy and of racial change, and the process of 'red-lining' (by which a red line was drawn around unacceptable areas for loans) became a symbol of racial discrimination and social injustice. Certainly, it had the effect of accelerating the rate of dilapidation in the inner-city built environment. Property was maintained poorly by owners and renters. The tax laws of the time also encouraged new construction rather than rehabilitation, so that many buildings were sold after their initial 10 years of tax relief, and this led to poor standards of construction and rapid deterioration. In the case of the road programmes, some were used to partition the inner-city zones and to isolate less socially acceptable groups: when it came to building inner-urban freeways, much older and lower-cost housing had to be demolished to make way for the roads, and then the raised highways provided a barrier between communities. These actions resulted in many protests, and some of the riots of the late 1960s were related to such events;

many sections of planned inner-urban freeways will never be built as a result.

Two more specific Federal programmes, designed to improve the inner-city environment, also resulted in the worsening of the lot of inner-city inhabitants. The shortage of housing for low-income groups was approached by an Act of 1937 which made it possible for the Federal government to fund the building (and later to subsidise the operation) of multifamily housing units for the needy. However, from the start this provision attracted the stigma associated with much of the 'welfare'-type of public policy in the United States. When the construction of such public housing was expanded after the Second World War, suburban neighbourhoods resisted it, and it was largely concentrated in inner-city areas until the US Supreme Court ruled this was unconstitutional in 1973. By this time the public housing projects had become synonymous with crime and vandalism, and some had even been pulled down a few years after construction for such reasons. In the early 1960s construction throughout the US was running at 20,000–40,000 units per year; this rose to over 100,000 units in the best year of 1970, but then declined rapidly; by 1977 only 6000 units were built and all President Carter's efforts to raise this made little impact. Such public housing now accounts for only 2 per cent of the total housing stock, and much of it is of poor and deteriorating quality. It has added to the poor housing available in the inner city.

The other development aimed at improving the inner-city environment during this period was that related to urban renewal and built into the 1949 Housing Act. The idea behind this provision was that many central areas of American cities were suffering from a combination of age and blight due to the shift away of some economic activities. Unsavoury commercial activities had turned sectors into 'skid-rows' and there was citizen pressure to clean up these undesirable areas. Urban renewal involved consolidation of the process under a single authority, funds for purchasing and demolishing old properties and for upgrading the infrastructure such as roads, and then permission to sell the cleared land for private industrial, commercial or residential development. This programme had a major impact on city centres across the United States, and led to the construction of grandiose city halls as well as having a major impact on the 'Manhattanisation' of many city centre areas. The central land increased in value as banks and other speculators bid for it to build high-rise office buildings. At the same time, low-income people were displaced, even from areas where rehabilitation would have been possible, and communities were broken up without concern for the rehousing of those displaced.

The impact of these Federal policies thus had the combined effect of encouraging suburban growth and the rebuilding of the city central business districts, but also of disrupting communities of low-income and minority groups. The social impact of these policies was particularly divisive and was worked out through the spatial separation of people into racial/income groups. Those left behind in the inner city had reduced access to employment opportunities. This separation was also made possible by the fragmented nature of local political divisions in many of the metropolitan areas: the control of the central city was divorced from that of the suburbs, and those living in the suburbs saw little reason for attempting to plan together. The central cities had the greatest social needs, but the high taxes put off businesses from taking up sites there and the tax base remained too low to cater for the needs of local residents and daily workers.

10.4 THE LOW-GROWTH CITIES OF THE 1970S

After the period of rapid population growth in the 1950s, and continuing growth above the national average during the 1960s, the large metropolitan centres in the United States grew only slowly during the 1970s. Some of those in the north-east lost population during this decade, and their inner cities became even more affected by neighbourhood abandonment and decline.

The 1970s witnessed a number of major changes in American population distribution. The natural rate of increase fell away as birth rates declined, the numbers of elderly increased, and there was a movement from metropolitan centres to rural places and small towns, paralleled by the Frostbelt-to-Sunbelt phenomenon. These changes were made possible by the extension of grant-aid infrastructure, electrical power and road access programmes to rural areas. Manufacturers discovered that labour was cheapest in these locations, and established small factories there. Black people in the unfriendly northern cities found that they could return south to retire or to take up some of the new jobs, and more black people moved out of the major cities than moved into them during this decade. This was a major cause of accelerated abandonment in central cities in the North, since new incomers did not replace those moving out and up the economic and social ladder.

Federal policies changed during this period to try and accommodate or reverse some of the previous mistakes. The urban renewal programme came to an end, and the public housing programme virtually ceased in inner cities. Subsidies were made available for the rehabilitation of inner-city properties, and tax reforms reduced the advantages to suburban developers. Clauses were built into the legislation to ensure that a proportion of low-cost housing should be built in all government-subsidised projects.

New approaches were also introduced. The Johnson administration established the cabinet-level Department of Housing and Urban Development in the late 1960s to focus attention on the needs of the inner cities: mortgages were provided for those wishing to rehabilitate older dwellings, and developers were subsidised to build low-cost housing, but this promising programme was terminated in 1973 after a number of financial scandals involving the private developers. Rents of poor families were subsidised. The Nixon administration in the early 1970s looked to local co-ordination and flexibility by introducing block grants to cover a series of aspects of urban change. The Community Development Act of 1974 established this approach, but there were difficulties in that too many places (including many suburbs) qualified for the funding at first. Special provisions had to be added to redirect funds to the inner cities, but even then much of the funding went to projects which developed recreational facilities and better-class housing. Nixon's other major innovation – the revenue-sharing programme whereby Federal funds were redistributed back to the states – also disadvantaged the worst inner-city situations by funnelling an undue proportion of the money to growing Sunbelt cities.

The Carter administration of the late 1970s set up the Urban Development Action Grant (UDAG) programme and insisted that 75 per cent of the funds went to central cities. This was more successful and also attracted matching private funds. By this stage also there was an effective rehabilitation programme, and many of the EDA projects were being centred in inner cities.

Thus, during this decade, there were greater and more appropriate efforts being made by the Federal government, but some were still misdirected (and benefited the well-off) and others had insufficient funding to make much difference to the very great social and economic problems of the inner cities. These were made more difficult during the decade by a combination of economic crises over energy supplies and the growing young population arising from the 'baby boom' years. The inner cities came to be seen as declining areas where the Federal government acted as a sort of caretaker. Private enterprise did not find worthwhile sources of investment in these declining areas, and the Federal government reflected the national conscience in supporting the services needed and cleaning up the degraded environment.

10.5 THE WITHDRAWAL OF FEDERAL INVOLVEMENT IN THE 1980S

The inability of Federal policies and programmes to come to terms with the problems of the central cities of America's major metropolitan areas in the 1970s caused President Reagan and his supporters to conclude that the decline of the inner cities was the fault of too many government and welfare payments. After 1980 it was the intention of the Reagan administration to remove the many supports available from the Federal government, and to turn this responsibility back to the states. Support for housing, infrastructure and welfare programmes would be affected in this way, and this would place the cities at a great disadvantage.

Relationships between state governments and the major cities had been so poor that the cities traditionally had related to the Federal government. State governments have lagged behind the Federal government in their levels of taxation, and most have not built up adequate bureaucracies to be able to administer the full range of services available through the Federal government. Moreover, a number of state governments were prevented from raising their tax levels by such measures as the famous 'Proposition 13' in California, which prohibited the state government from increasing taxation.

However, it was not a straightforward matter of the president's decision, and the US Congress was loath to rescind legislation of the kind that helped people in the constituencies. There have been reductions in funding for the programmes favouring the inner city, but few programmes have been ended.

The Reagan administration also introduced the concept of Urban Enterprise Zones, in which tax incentives were provided for the rebuilding of blighted areas and private investment in industrial parks. Tax credits were available for the hiring of long-term unemployed people. There were proposals for some remission of safety and air quality standards, and also of minimum wage provisions to try and encourage new employment opportunities. But such measures are difficult to get through the US Congress, and although the Senate passed Bills on three occasions, the House of Representatives was still unhappy about them in 1985.

10.6 CONCLUSIONS

The experience of the metropolitan areas in the United States provides some important insights to the relationship of Federal government programmes with economic and social change. It could be said that the changing form of the big-city environment is a product of dominant economic forces. If so, the Federal government programmes have hardly been able to touch the major problems which have arisen. The attempts to abolish poverty in the 1960s have given way to an acceptance of it in the 1980s.

However, it is also clear that certain Federal programmes had an impact on urban form by encouraging suburban living for the middle and upper classes from 1950 onwards. It was this movement which separated the poor from the rich and created many of the modern problems of the inner city. It would probably have happened without government encouragement, but that certainly hurried the changes along and may have helped to create the sense of well-being which gave rise to the baby boom and demographic instability.

11.   Conclusions: Regions and Regionalism

11.1 INTRODUCTION

Regional studies are returning to geographical enquiry as a central part of that discipline. An earlier descriptive approach to regions, responding to the innate curiosity that people have about other parts of the world, became intellectually stagnant. Attempts to develop a subject of greater academic interest lurched firstly into attempts to make geography a behavioural science, and then into a focus on individual personal feelings and contributions to locational decision-making. These attempts were partial in application, but in the 1980s there has been a new thrust in which geography is able to contribute a central role to social understanding (Lee, 1985) through its broad spatial, environmental and global perspectives. This approach incorporates regional analysis and an understanding of regionalism.

This final chapter brings together the earlier discussion and studies in the book, and provides a basis for other related work. The relationship of such changing ideas to the United States in particular has been a fruitful study, since it has made it possible to emphasise many of the issues involved in regional analysis and regionalism in the context of a large nation. Although many of the features of economy, politics and society are unique to the United States, others are applicable elsewhere, and many of the general ideas emerging from this study should be transferable to other nations.

In this book a distinction has been drawn between the more academic form of regional studies and applications of the regional concept in regionalism – both informally and in formal public policy. To date there has been a gap between theory and models derived from academic studies and the public policy attempts to influence change through region-based programmes (House, 1983).

11.2 A FRAMEWORK FOR REGIONAL STUDIES

The geographer is now able to build on the descriptive base for regional studies with a range of analytical tools and the beginnings of explanatory theory.

11.2.1 Regional description

The descriptive base has been broadened due to the development of the findings of analytical studies in more systematic aspects of economic, social and political geography, and this has turned attention away from the former simplistic and deterministic emphasis on the interaction between human societies and their natural environments. Spatial differences are now seen (House, 1983) to be the result of:

(1) Varied conditions of natural and human resources. The differences of climate, relief, water and mineral resources and position have been important factors in producing a varied mosaic of regions within the US, as have the groups of people, both those indigenous and those arriving and settling specific areas.

(2) Varied ways in which groups of people have interpreted and exploited their position and resources. Clearly, the aboriginal inhabitants of North America had different views of the natural and human resources from those of subsequent colonists from Europe and used them in different ways which gave rise to varied patterns of regional geography.

(3) Varied courses of economic development and stages reached. Some parts of the US became industrialised ahead of others, and there are clear differences between the older manufacturing areas and those with newer factories. Some parts of the nation show signs of economic growth, while others are in decline. Patterns of regional variations are dynamic, not static.

(4) Significant features of regional differences may be related to

the institutional, social or political cultures which affect economic change. Within the US, despite the overall national context, there are a number of regional variations of this type which can be recognised. They are part of the historical legacy of cultural development.

(5) The nature and rate of regional change and adjustment inside the US are also conditioned by influences external to the nation. No nation in the late twentieth century is an island, divorced from world affairs, and the regional geography of the US has been affected by external influences since the arrival of Columbus in 1492. The initial orientation to Europe has been changed for a central world position with increasing interactions southwards to Latin America and westwards to the Pacific and Asia (as well as northwards to Canada).

Points (1) and (2) formed the basis of Chapter 2, and points (3) to (5) of Chapters 3 and 4. These characteristics of regional differences provide an enhanced view for the merely curious, but also contribute to further studies.

11.2.2 Regional analysis

By 'analysis' we mean the deeper probing of relationships within geographical regions. Whereas description allows us to answer 'where?' and 'when?' questions, analysis asks 'how?' questions. It seeks to answer them by establishing relationships between the features of a region and the human activities taking place. Strictly, 'analysis' is the taking apart of aspects of a subject for more detailed consideration, and this is what happens to establish these relationships. It is the aim of geographical studies to bring together the results of analysis in the process of 'synthesis'. In order to do this it is necessary to establish an understanding of the environmental and social structures and the processes associated with them. Then the impacts of fresh human actions can be assessed against this context: 'place' and 'people' are brought together and their interactions give rise to changes in the environmental and social structure. This is a complex, dynamic set of processes without any inevitable outcomes, and involves both history and geography. It has been termed the 'geography of transformation' (Lee, 1985), involving a set of basic understandings:

(1) Of the functioning of social processes, both regular and irregular, to create, transform and recreate society. The understanding of processes (e.g. of industrial production and the division of labour) is important in relation to the understanding of how locational decisions are reached. By this means geographical space becomes an integral part of industrial production.

(2) Of the relationships between day-to-day actions and social structures. Individuals live in the context of a set of social structures, but can modify them to a certain extent. The actions of individuals are thus not mercilessly determined by a social system, but they are imbued with personal responsibility and possibilities for instigating change – within the context of time and space.

(3) Of the nature of social transformation, which involves the role of the individual – created by social forces and yet able to recreate them.

(4) Of the ways in which geographical space affects social practice and acts as an essential medium for it. This places geographical study and analysis at the centre of reshaping the world, and regional geography at the centre of geographical study.

Regional study in this context becomes a matter of the interactions described above, and of different levels of 'regions' – local/urban, subnational and global. The region itself is an active medium, not just a setting: 'the spatial perimeter and physical environment are mobilised as part of the interaction, and become a factor of which the actors are aware' (Lee, 1985). Regions are constantly being constructed, destroyed and reconstructed as local and non-local processes of social development interact within that particular section of the earth's surface. Real places and real people – not shadowy ideals or norms – are the basis for this type of study. These themes have been developed in Chapters 3 and 4 in particular, but are also relevant to Chapters 5 to 10.

Thus, the subjects for analysis are the people involved in decision-making, the nature and constraints of the social system and environmental endowment, and the processes at work in human economic, social and political activities. The synthesis of these strands aims at providing a realistic and holistic study of sections of the earth's surface – or regional geography.

11.2.3 The explanation of regional differences

The study of regions implies differences. Another way of approaching this is as the geography of uneven development. Explanations attempt to answer the most difficult questions: those beginning with 'why?'. At present, only an outline framework can be suggested for explanations of uneven development.

The main global political-economic system is that of capitalism, or the free market economy, and this is developed most fully in the United States. The basic tenet of this system is to produce a surplus, or profit, for reinvestment and the promotion of further economic growth, and in so doing to increase the personal wealth of the owners of the means of production. This has a number of results which give rise to uneven development at various levels of geographical scale (Smith, 1984):

(1) Natural resources are regarded as having a value in relation to the market: natural forces are controlled and natural substances extracted to become the raw materials for manufacture into goods of higher value. This has the effect of altering the relationship between humans and their natural environment: in the 'primitive' stage of society people survived and developed their social systems in co-operation with nature; when non-human beings and matter came to be regarded as commodities, an alienation between humans and the natural world occurred, and this was enhanced by the switch from societies dominated by agricultural production to those dominated by manufacturing production. Eventually all 'nature' comes to have an exchange value imposed on it in relation to marketplace norms, and even places like the Yellowstone National Park are 'produced environments' with wildlife management and altered landscapes – subject to the economic demands of tourists and environmentalists.

(2) Society is divided into classes, distinguished by their relationship to processes of production and marketing. Those

who control these processes obtain additional profits by 'creaming off' what is really earned by the workers, or producers. This division is important in an understanding of uneven development, since there is an important association between class and residential location.

(3) Geographical space becomes differentiated into places on the basis of these economic, social and political processes. The wealth created by economic activity tends to be concentrated in some areas and not others, and these areas of concentrated capital accumulation stand out from areas with little. The most economic sites for production are differentiated from the least economic, giving rise to regions of growth and to lagging regions.

These features of capitalist societies have different effects at different scales. At the scale of the major urban centre there has been a differentiation of workplace and residence since the early part of the factory era. The ground-rent system controls the distribution of land uses, concentrating the high-value uses (especially with tall office blocks) in the central business district. These high-value areas are surrounded by low-value inner-city areas of old and declining worker housing inhabited by the poorest groups. Then there is a suburban zone of competition for sites for industrial, commercial and residential use.

There is usually an attempt made through urban planning to reduce conflicts of interest which occur due to the market-based allocation of urban land, and in order to reduce the impacts of such allocations on the disadvantaged (which might lead to civil unrest). In American cities it has been seen (Chapters 7 and 10) that the political base of decision-making often reflects the major 'marketplace' interests, particularly in the urban sectors experiencing economic growth. Regulations for land use favour the middle and upper classes. Disadvantaged groups may control inner-city areas (as the number of black mayors shows), but seldom possess the resources from the tax base to make changes they would like to (Johnston, 1982).

Within each nation there are divisions into regions which tend to fluctuate in prosperity. Some regions have the advantage over others at one stage, and experience economic growth, when they attract capital investment to build infrastructure and production facilities. This draws in people to work in the growth industries. The process then ties down the capital investment and immobilises it in the built environment of roads, factories and houses. If locational advantages shift with changes of fashion or other ways in which economies are altered, the initially-advantaged region then experiences decline. Its economy may find it difficult to reorientate to the new circumstances, due to so much investment in the buildings and transport facilities required for the earlier stage. Other regions become more attractive to new investment for greatest profit and shifts take place. Regional differences within a nation thus experience a see-saw of uneven development. This can be applied easily to the United States, and examples have been discussed in Chapters 3, 5, 6 and 7.

When the global scale is considered, the whole world is now, viewed as a potential market: not only have places with former non-monetary economies been brought into the same realm, but also places with centrally-planned economies, such as those in eastern Europe and China, find it difficult to cut themselves off from such processes. This might be expected to be having the effect of equalising conditions on the world scale, although there might be some debate as to whether this is a levelling down, or a levelling up process. There is also a long way to go before economic circumstances of the developing nations equal those of the United States!

The point is that the socio-economic processes at work in the free market or capitalist system are responsible for the differentiation into the developed and underdeveloped worlds, the subnational regions of growth or decline and the differences between the suburbs and the inner cities. Although this is an essentially Marxist explanation, and therefore usually tied into a corollary of inevitable revolutionary action to put things right, it is not necessary to link the two parts of this equation. The explanation may be helpful in other ways in leading towards an understanding of other aspects of national and international planning.

Within the United States it is clear that attempts to plan within the urban or regional context to change the current situation have to come to terms with the tenets of the free-market system. Aims which are linked to economic growth tend to be more realistic than those which are related to the achievement of equal opportunities for all people. This explanation of regional differences thus informs the ways in which regionalism is likely to be successful.

11.3 A FRAMEWORK FOR REGIONALISM

Although there are more informal types of regionalism, most of them lead towards the involvement of public policy action at the subnational scale. In the United States the context of such public policy is extremely complex. The point has been made at the beginning of Chapter 8 that the US political environment maintains a conservative stance over long periods of time with infrequent 'windows of opportunity' for more interventionist action by the Federal government. Within such a large nation there are also regional differences in political outlook which can be characterised in general terms. House (1983) quotes Elazar's categorisation of political cultures: the 'individualistic', in which all government is seen as purely utilitarian in value and politics is a matter of responding to public pressure, is strong in the north-eastern manufacturing belt area; the 'moralistic', which seeks the good of society, expects the government to promote the general welfare, and is strong in the territory from New England west to the northern Great Lakes; and the 'traditionalistic', which involves aspects of elitism and paternalism and a government devoted to maintaining the social order, is still evident in the American South. These basic attitudes were transferred west across the Mississippi in various combinations and with modifications, but are often engrained in large numbers of people in the eastern regions of prime association with these characteristics.

Not only is there a variety of regional expressions of political attitudes, but there have also been shifts over time in the relative national importance of these views. The 1930s, and to some extent the 1940s, provided a limited period in which the moralistic approach gave rise to welfare legislation and such regional projects as TVA. During the 1920s and 1950s the individualistic, business-oriented approach was dominant and inhibited central government action; TVA bent to its will; and it has returned again in the 1980s. The 1960s especially, and the 1970s to a more limited extent, also provided a phase of the moralistic approach, spawning welfare, regional and environmental policies at the Federal level. Although the traditionalistic approach did not succeed in gaining national power during this phase, it continued to be important in the South with its one-party system until the 1970s.

Thus, the American political environment is always changing

and containing a wide range of views concerning the desirability of public intervention. This is why there has been so little regional planning. What little regional planning has managed to emerge from the processes of public policy has been limited in scope and funding, and few commentators had credited it with any great success. It is always initially difficult to get such programmes on the public policy agenda. In many cases, as surveyed in Chapters 8 and 9, the public policies were inappropriate (TVA, ARA, EDA and the Title V Regional Commissions), or had little funding, or both. This lack of success has been viewed as an inevitable outcome of the American free-market society, and its thrust of encouraging economic growth rather than of assisting the weak (Dowd, 1977; Whisnant, 1980). Such a view has often led to a 'holier-than-thou' opting out of attempts to find distinctive American solutions to the issues addressed by regionalism in its various guises.

In addition to the shifting ground of political support for public intervention, both regionally and over time, there has also been a shift in the nature of lagging regions. In mid century they were essentially rural in character, but by the 1960s the inner-urban zones were taking over the unenviable position of harbouring the greatest majority of the nation's poor. Although there were some shifts in public policy programmes to this end (particularly with the reorientation of the EDA), the result was for the legislation of the 1960s to appear out of phase with needs by the late 1970s. President Reagan was able to convince many that this meant the programmes were fundamentally wrong and that they should be cut back or ended. The partial nature and gradual development of many programmes also produced a largely unco-ordinated range of different regions based on public policies.

And yet it is clear that many of the difficulties in American society have a spatial dimension. Both unduly rapid growth, and economic stagnation and decline, require planning guidance and investment to ease the difficulties for particular areas. Some problems are national in scope, but many are regional or local. The American political system based on states and local governments was established over 200 years ago in an age of very different scales of personal mobility, and other scales of unit are more appropriate in the late twentieth century. Regional groupings of states, and local groupings of counties and municipalities, after the fashion of ARC, might provide a more flexible base for linking local needs with state concerns and federal funding sources.

11.4 REGIONS AND REGIONALISM IN THE UNITED STATES

In linking the academic analysis and explanations to the pragmatic needs expressed in regionalism, a number of conflicts have to be faced. Attempts to establish theoretical models by the social sciences have not been successful in terms of their use within public policy to date (Zysman, 1980). However, it is the tension between the academic and the practical which is a test of the usefulness of concepts such as those of the region and regionalism in the reduction of social conflicts.

The first of the conflicts which arise from these considerations is that between equity, efficiency and the improvement of the quality of life. The philosophies of Americans provide the conflict here: individualists would accept that inequalities are inevitable and that the individual has an opportunity (and even a responsibility) to take advantage of the system to 'get on' in efforts to increase overall efficiency. A further point made by those who take this line is that regional disequilibrium is temporary, and market forces will eventually produce balanced conditions across the nation. Those who are poor have only themselves to blame according to many Americans. The moralists believe that there is the possibility of improving equality of opportunity for all without sacrificing efficiency, and perhaps it is even worth doing that to an extent if overall quality of life can be improved. A more radical view is that inequality is inevitable within the capitalistic system, and that this is also inefficient and damaging to the general quality of life: environmental pollution is seen as a necessary outcome of producing the greatest surplus of capital.

Secondly, there is often a conflict between national and regional (or local) needs – at least as perceived by the local people. This occurred with the TVA programme in the 1930s and since. Federal legislation is inevitably related to the whole nation, rather than to its parts; the states tend to be concerned with their internal affairs, as do counties and municipalities. This leaves areas of need at particular spatial scales which the current system finds it difficult to address.

Thirdly, there is a continuing debate as to whether government intervention is either necessary or useful. President Reagan has been able to persuade most of the voters in presidential elections on two occasions in the 1980s that less government is desirable. Although a number of studies (Schwartz, 1983) have exposed the fallacy of this position, it is not easy to change attitudes which have become engrained in the minds of many Americans.

Fourthly, even if government intervention is allowed as a possible solution to regional differences, there is a further debate as to whether there should be assistance for investment to stimulate the economic growth of particular places by 'bricks and mortar' programmes, or whether it is better to invest in people by programmes of education, health and other types of welfare. The American predilection has been for the more tangible infrastructure programmes. This conflict also emphasises another important point. By and large both regional and urban planning give rise to the production of physical infrastructure such as roads, houses, water systems, schools, hospitals. Any efforts (such as the initial objectives of TVA) to engage in social engineering as part of planning have been failures to date. It appears that people who live in planned towns or suburbs have different ideas from the planners on what they wish to do with the built environment. In any case, the built environment is produced at 'one short period of time, whereas society changes and thus reacts with it in different ways.

Finally, there is also debate concerning the nature of the type of region which is most suitable in this context of evening out differences within a nation such as the United States. Large metropolitan regions are one possibility, and others are the local regions such as the LDDs of ARC or the EDDs of EDA (containing several counties). Then there are the larger regions, including those adopted for the regional commissions such as ARC (containing parts or all of several states). Even when the size of a regional base for planning or co-ordination (or whatever process is appropriate) is determined, it has to be remembered that regions are interdependent within a nation and that nations are interdependent within the global context. Perhaps a hierarchy of such regions within the nations might be most suitable.

Can a study such as this book suggest a way forward? It is at least worth pointing out that the only pattern which has combined aims of equity, efficiency and quality of life with an integration of federal, regional, state and local interests, and a variety of types of grant-aid programmes to stimulate both human resource and physical infrastructure development, is that of the Appalachian

Regional Commission. There are still voices to be heard in Washington DC which would suggest that a nationwide set of multistate regions with related multicounty local districts could be established to encourage economic growth across the US – in both growing and lagging regions. Today's growth region may be tomorrow's lagging region.

The ARC pattern also makes it possible to have local expressions of need related to regional, state and national needs. It provides for the involvement of locally elected officials, state politicians and the US Congress, together with the business community and other residents. The ARC LDDs have demonstrated that the mix of business people, elected officials and other local interests can have positive impacts in terms of co-operation, involvement and a wider view of patterns of change in the region and nation. The experimental work has been carried out, and it may be easier to implement in the late 1980s than it was in 1979 when this suggestion was last debated in the US Congress. Since that time the Title V Commissions have been disbanded, and the strengths of other agencies reduced, and so the pressures to devise a system on the basis of the bizarre boundaries chosen for those Commissions have gone.

Bibliography

This bibliography refers to those works consulted in the writing of this book. They contain further bibliographies which will lead the reader deeper into the literature on this subject.

Bennett, C. F. (1983). *Conservation and Management of Natural Resources in the United States* (Wiley: New York)

Berkman, R. L. and Viscusi, W. K. (1973). *Damming the West: Ralph Nader's study group report on the Bureau of Reclamation* (Grossman: New York)

Birdsall, S. S. and Florin, J. W. (1978). *Regional Landscapes of the United States and Canada* (Wiley: New York)

Bradshaw, M. J. (1982). 'Federal initiatives and regionalism: with special reference to Appalachia', in *Regions and Regionalism in the United States: Past and Present*, ed. C. Brookeman (American Studies Resources Centre: Polytechnic of Central London)

Bradshaw, M. J. (1984a). 'The impact of federal policies in Appalachia, USA', unpublished PhD thesis, Department of Geography, University of Leicester

Bradshaw, M. J. (1984b). 'TVA at fifty', *Geography*, 69, 209–20

Bradshaw, M. J. (1985). 'Public policy in Appalachia: the application of a neglected geographical factor?' *Transactions of the Institute of British Geographers*, ns, 10, 385–400

Brunn, S. D. and Wheeler, J. O. (1980). *The American Metropolitan System: Present and Future* (Arnold: London)

Bunge, W. (1975). 'Detroit humanly viewed: the American urban present', in *Human Geography in a Shrinking World*, ed. R. Abler *et al.* (Duxbury: Belmont, California)

Caudill, H. (1962). *Night Comes to the Cumberlands* (Atlantic–Little, Brown: Boston)

Clark, D. (1985). *Post-industrial America* (Methuen: London)

Clark, G. L., Gertler, M. S. and Whiteman, T. (1986). *Regional Development: Studies in Adjustment Theory* (Allen & Unwin: London)

Cox, K. R. (1972). *Man, Location and Behaviour: an Introduction to Human Geography* (Wiley: New York)

Davies, C. S. (1983). 'The imprint of federal policy on evolving urban form', in *United States Public Policy: a Geographical View*, ed. J. W. House (Oxford University Press)

Dowd, D. F. (1977). *The Twisted Dream: Capitalist Development in the United States since 1776* (Winthrop: Cambridge, Mass)

Estall, R. (1982). 'Planning in Appalachia: an examination of the Appalachian regional development programme and its implications for the future of the American Regional Planning Commissions', *Transactions of the Institute of British Geographers*, ns, 7, 35–58

Fellmeth, R. C. (1973). *The Politics of Land: Ralph Nader's Study Group Report on Land use in California* (Grossman, New York)

Fox, K. (1985). *Metropolitan America: Urban Life and Urban Policy in the United States, 1940–1980* (Macmillan: London)

Friedmann, J. and Weaver, C. (1979). *Territory and Function* (Arnold: London)

Gottman, J. (1961). *Megalopolis* (Twentieth Century Fund: New York)

Gould, P. and White, R. (1986). *Mental Maps* (Allen & Unwin: London)

Gregory, D. (1985). 'People, places and practices: the future of human geography', in *Geographical Futures*, ed. R. King (Geographical Association: Sheffield)

Guinness P. and Bradshaw, M. J. (1985). *North America: a human geography*. Hodder & Stoughton: London)

Hart, J. (1982). 'The highest form of the geographer's art', *Annals of the Association of American Geographers* 72, 1–29

House, J. W. (1983). 'Regional and area development', in *United States Public Policy: a Geographical View*, ed. J. W. House (Oxford University Press)

Issel, W. (1985). *Social Change in the United States, 1945–1983* (Macmillan: London)

Johnson, R. (1977). *The Central Arizona Project 1918–1968* (University of Arizona Press: Tucson, Arizona)

Johnston, R. J. (1982). *The American Urban System: a Geographical Perspective* (Longman: London)

Kahrl, W. L. (1978). *The California Water Atlas* (State of California)

Lee, R. (1985). 'The future of the region: regional geography as education for transformation', in *Geographical Futures*, ed. R. King (Geographical Association: Sheffield)

Lynch, D. F., Lantis, D. W. and Pearson, R. W. (1981). 'Alaska: land and resource issues', *Focus*, 31, 3

Meinig, D. W. (1972). 'American Wests: preface to a geographical interpretation', *Annals of the Association of American Geographers*, 62, 159–84

Michener, J. (1978). *Chesapeake* (Corgi Books: London)

Michener, J. (1985). Texas (Secker & Warburg: London)

Morrill, R. L. and Wohlenburg, E. H. (1971). *The Geography of Poverty* (McGraw-Hill: New York)

O'Hare, W. (1985). *Poverty in America: Trends and New Patterns* (Population Reference Bureau: Washington DC)

Paterson, J. H. (1982). 'Regions and regionalism: past and present', in *Regions and Regionalism: Past and Present*, ed. C. Brookeman (American Studies Resources Centre: Polytechnic of Central London)

Paterson, J. H. (1984). *North America* (Oxford University Press)

Patterson, J. T. (1981). *The Struggle against Poverty in America 1939–1980* (Harvard University Press: Cambridge, Mass)

Rostow, W. W. (1977). 'Regional change in the Fifth Kondratieff Upswing', in *The Rise of the Sunbelt Cities*, ed. D. C. Perry and A. J. Watkins (Sage: London)

Schwarz, J. E. (1983). *America's Hidden Success: a Reassessment of Twenty Years of Public Policy* (W. W. Norton: New York)

Smith, D. (1973). *The Geography of Social Well-being in the United States* (McGraw-Hill: New York)

Smith, N. (1984). *Uneven Development* (Blackwell: Oxford)

Starkey, O. R., Robinson, J. L. and Miller, C. S. (1975). *The Anglo-American Realm* (McGraw-Hill; New York)

Stilgoe, J. R. (1982). *Common Landscape of America, 1580–1845* (Yale University Press: New Haven, Conn)

US Bureau of the Census (1984). *Statistical Abstract of the United States 1985* (Government Printing Office: Washington, DC)

US Congress (1979). *Hearings before the Subcommittee on Economic Development of the Committee on Public Works, US Senate. 94-H8* (Government Printing Office: Washington, DC)

Whisnant, D. (1980). *Modernizing the Mountaineer* (Appalachian Consortium Press: Boone, NC)

White, E. L., Foscue, E. J. and McKnight, T. L. (1979). *Regional Geography of Anglo-America* (Prentice-Hall: New Jersey)

Wilson, D. E. (1980). *The National Planning Idea in United States Public Policy* (Westview: Boulder, Colorado)

Winsburg, M. D. (1986). 'Geographical polarization of whites and minorities in large US cities: 1960–1980' *Population Today* (March 1986), 6–7

Yeates, M. (1980). *North American Urban Patterns* (Arnold: London)

Zelinsky, W. (1973). *The Cultural Geography of the United States* (Prentice-Hall: New Jersey)

Zelinsky, W. (1980). 'North America's vernacular regions', *Annals of the Association of American Geographers*, 70, 1–16

Zysman, J. (1980). 'Research, politics and policy: regional planning in America', in *The Utilization of the Social Sciences in Policy-Making in the USA* (OECD: Paris)

Reference has also been made to the publications of Congressional Quarterly Inc. (Washington, DC), including the Weekly Report and annual Almanac, and also the series, *Congress and the Nation, 1945–1980*, vols I–V.

Index